# Poetry Play Any Day
## With
# Jane Yolen

Cheryl Potts

Alleyside Press®

Fort Atkinson, Wisconsin

## Also by Cheryl Potts

*Poetry Galore and More With Shel Silverstein*
*Poetry Fun by the Ton With Jack Prelutsky*
*Poetry Time with Dr. Seuss Rhyme*

Published by Alleyside Press, an imprint of Highsmith Press
Highsmith Press
W5527 Highway 106
P.O. Box 800
Fort Atkinson, Wisconsin 53538-0800
**1-800-558-2110**

© Cheryl Potts, 1999
Cover design: Bill Higby

**Library of Congress Cataloging-in-Publication Data**
    Potts, Cheryl, 1953-
        Poetry play any day with Jane Yolen / Cheryl Potts.
            p.  cm.
        Includes bibliographical references (p.  ).
        ISBN 0-57950-038-2 (pbk. : alk. paper)
        1. Language arts (Elementary) 2. Poetry--Study and teaching
    (Elementary)  I. Yolen, Jane.  II. Title.
    LB1576.P683 1999
    372.64--DC21                                          99-29784
                                                              CIP

# Contents

## Once Upon Ice

## An Invitation to the Butterfly Ball

## Elfabet

## Welcome to the Green House

## Weather Report

# Introduction

Each school year, teachers and librarians are faced with the difficult task of motivating children to read. Not only do we strive to provide age-appropriate, stimulating and quality literature, but further, we challenge our students to become "life-long learners." Now more than ever, we have become self-esteem builders, motivators and, at times, attitude-changers of children who have reading difficulties. These challenges create a never-ending demand for supportive, innovative and creative activities to build literacy skills.

*Poetry Play Any Day with Jane Yolen* was created for the elementary teacher who likes to interact and be involved in the learning process of his or her students. This book was designed to create enthusiasm, appreciation and excitement for rhyme and rhythm in poetry as well as to reinforce reading, writing and language skills. It will also introduce students to the forms and styles of poetry and provide a nonthreatening, low-key, fun approach for students to experiment and practice poetry writing. Jane Yolen's books of poetry create springboards for many classroom activities, ideas and projects because of her diverse themes and topics.

You may think of this book as an author study which includes hands-on activities and ideas that will enhance your regular, whole language or literacy programs. Wherever possible other literature links are listed to expand the theme or topic study. Many of the games and projects included here are or can be adapted to other grade levels.

# About Jane Yolen

Jane Yolen was born in New York, New York, on February 11, 1939. She received her B.A. from Smith College and her M.Ed. from the University of Massachusetts.

Both of Jane's parents were writers — her father a journalist, her mother a short story writer. Jane started very young as a poet and writer of songs. Her first experience was writing a class musical in first grade. It was all about vegetables and she played the Chief Carrot. "We all ended up in a salad together."

In junior high, she wrote a class essay about New York State manufacturing in rhyming verse. In college, Jane wrote her final exam in American Intellectual History in rhyme and got an A+ from a very surprised teacher.

Jane feels that all the books that she's ever read have inspired her own writing. Her parents were very supportive of her efforts and that inspired her as well. She recalls riding with her mother and baby brother on the bus to the Virginia public library during World War II and reading books on the way home.

Jane and her husband have three grown children. They divide their time between homes in Massachusetts and Scotland.

Jane Yolen is the author of more than 160 books for children and adults. She has numerous awards: ALA Notable Books, SCBWI Golden Kite Award in 1974, Christopher Medal in 1978, the Garden State Children's Book Award in 1981 and the Mythopoeic Society Aslan Award in 1984. She has also received the Kerlan Award for children's literature, the Regina Medal for her body of work, and the World Fantasy Award. In addition, her book *Piggins* won the Charlotte Award and many of her books have received Parents' Choice Awards and honor citations.

She has three pieces of advice for young writers, "One: read, read, read! You must read a wide range of books. Two: write, write, write! Keep a journal, write letters, anything to keep the 'writing muscles' in shape. Three: don't let anyone stop you from writing. Be persistent no matter what critical editors have to say about your writing."

 Activity One

# ABC Sequence Poems

Introduce your students to Jane Yolen's *Alphabestiary* and *All in the Woodland Early.* Since these ABC books picture different animals beginning with each letter of the alphabet, they make a great springboard into writing ABC poems. Display other ABC books in your classroom for students to read and browse for ideas.

For enrichment fun, introduce your students to ABC sequence poems. They are an acrostic poem using any sequence of five letters in the alphabet. This kind of poem expresses feelings such as: happiness, excitement, fear, anger, etc.

### Rules for writing ABC sequence poems:

1. You need five lines.
2. The five lines use words or phrases to explain your feelings or mood.
3. The first letter of each word in the line is in alphabetical order, but they do not have to start with "A."
4. The last line should be a complete sentence.

Model this poem activity on the chalkboard or chart paper and allow students to share their ideas together at first. Leave the sample up and encourage students to try one on their own. Here are some examples:

O off to the zoo
P patiently waiting at the gate
Q quickly finding our way          **or**
R running out of breath
S seals are fun to watch!

H hurry, hurry, it's hot
I I can't stand it
J jump in the pool
K kick and splash
L Let's jump in the pool again!

## A to Z Poem

### ★ For Older Students

For older students, using the complete alphabet to compose an A to Z poem is a bigger challenge. Students may want to use their dictionary or thesaurus to complete this task. However, it can cover a variety of topics such as pets, people, toys, food, Christmas, school, etc.

### Guidelines:

1. Use your topic as the title of the poem.
2. Words or phrases related to the topic are used in alphabetical order, A to Z.
3. If you have trouble with the letter "x," you may use words like "ex"tra or "ex"cited.

**Examples:**

### *Christmas*

Angels, bows, cookies, dolls, eggnog, fancy garland,

holiday, icicles, jack-in-the-box,

kissing, loved Mom's necklace, ornaments,

purple quilt, really sleepy, tinsel, unusual velvet wallet,

exhausted, yawning, zonked.

### *Roller Coaster*

Anxious, brave, curious, dangerous, eager, fantastic,

get-going, hallelujah, ignorant, jerk, kook, lurch,

madness, nausea, orbit, paranoid, quit, reflex, sick,

terminal, unforgettable, violent, weak, exhale, yoyo,

zombie.

Display the finished ABC or A to Z poems around your classroom and urge students to read them. These poems would also make a wonderful classroom poetry book. Encourage students to illustrate their poems and save their creations in a poetry folder or book for the whole school year.

 Activity Two

# Rhyming

Take several days to enjoy reading Jane Yolen's poem book titled *What Rhymes with Moon?* Choose two or three of the poems, make copies for each child and ask†them to underline the rhyming words. For instance, in "The Moon Is a Sickle" the rhyming words are stars–Mars and sky–why. Remind students that rhyming words sound the same at the end of the word but they do not have to be spelled the same. For example, in the poem "Some Say," "green" and "seen" rhyme and are spelled the same whereas "stare" and "there" rhyme but are not spelled the same. To give students additional practice in locating rhyming words, use the following poems from *What Rhymes with Moon?*: "Cutting Hair"; "Dream Maker"; "Green Cheese"; "Father Wolf's Midnight Song"; "Mama, Mama, Catch Me a Star"; "Christmas Eve: Hatfield."

Depending on the grade level, read the poems orally as students listen and underline the rhyming words, or use this as an independent activity.

# Creating Their Own List

**★ For Older Students**

If students are able to identify rhyming words in a poem, ask them to write a list of rhyming words. Using the theme of "moon" from Yolen's book title, have students brainstorm and write a list of words that rhyme. Record these words on chart paper to use in activity three. Start by asking students to write down one-syllable words that rhyme with "moon," such as tune, dune, June, loon, spoon, goon, noon. Then, list possible two-syllable words, such as: balloon, raccoon, bassoon, harpoon, buffoon, saloon, baboon, etc.

Set this chart aside and give students additional opportunities to write rhyming word lists by creating **picture-rhyming cards**. Cut out magazine or calendar pictures that would elicit rhyming words by the action or subject shown in the picture. For example, cut out a picture that shows a deer, snake, bear, goat, shell, mouse, whale, cat, seal, owl, fall, spring, etc. Mount these pictures on colored construction paper and label each (laminate for durability). Then, attach a blank sheet of paper below the picture so that students can add rhyming words. Display the picture-rhyming cards on a bulletin board for students to work on during their free time.

You may also want to challenge students to try rhyming two-syllable words. Mount pictures (same as above) for students to write on. Picture possibilities are: bunny, bicycle, cherry, rocket, daisy, balloon, peeling, riding, jumping, etc.

### Sample rhyming words:

| | |
|---|---|
| deer | *steer, here, near, dear, clear, fear, spear, tear* |
| goat | *coat, boat, float, tote, note, bloat, wrote, throat* |
| shell | *bell, well, tell, sell, yell, spell, smell, gel* |
| whale | *hail, trail, sale, male, mail, nail, fail* |
| seal | *meal, deal, real, feel, kneel, peel, heel* |
| owl | *growl, prowl, fowl, towel, howl, trowel* |
| fall | *mall, tall, small, ball, call, hall, wall* |
| spring | *ring, ding, king, sing, wing, bring, thing* |
| bunny | *funny, honey, sunny, runny* |
| bicycle | *tricycle, icicle* |
| cherry | *berry, fairy, dairy, merry, hairy, very, wary* |
| daisy | *lazy, crazy, hazy* |
| balloon | *raccoon, baboon, bassoon, harpoon* |
| peeling | *ceiling, healing, dealing, feeling, kneeling, wheeling* |
| riding | *sliding, deciding, colliding, gliding, siding, chiding* |
| jumping | *thumping, dumping, slumping, pumping* |

Cat

| sat | mat |
|---|---|
| hat | bat |
| fat | pat |
| rat | flat |
| blat | |

 Activity Three

# Couplets

After modeling and practicing with rhyming words, guide students on how to write couplets. A couplet is a simple, two-line poem that rhymes. Most couplets are funny, but they don't have to be. Using the chart of words rhymed with "moon" from activity two, share examples of rhyming couplets. <u>Leave out the last rhyming word</u> and ask students to figure out the missing word.

**Example:**

My friend and I wrote a musical <u>tune</u>.
I sang the words and he played the (<u>bassoon</u>).

I went to the zoo and bought a <u>balloon</u>.
At the monkey cage it was grabbed by a (<u>baboon</u>).

School is out the middle of <u>June</u>.
We'll celebrate summer at quarter past (<u>noon</u>).

To capture a whale you'd use a <u>harpoon</u>.
But you'd need a net to catch a (<u>raccoon</u>).

In the nursery rhyme, the cow jumped over the <u>moon</u>.
Then the dish ran away with the (<u>spoon</u>).

### ★ For Older Students

Older students may be able to write rhyming couplets independently. Ask them to write any two words of their choice that rhyme. Allow them time to write their couplets, then share them orally. Here are some rhyming words to get them started:

pickle – nickel, chilly – silly, rocket – pocket, sliding – colliding, lobster – mobster, copy – sloppy, daisy – lazy, bird – heard, power – tower, tomatoes – potatoes.

---

**Additional Resources**

Asch, Frank. *Happy Birthday Moon*. Prentice-Hall, 1982.

———. *Mooncake*. Scholastic, 1983.

———. *Moongame*. Prentice-Hall, 1984.

———. *Moonbear's Books*. Houghton Mifflin, 1997.

Babcock, Chris. *No Moon, No Milk*. Scholastic, 1993.

Brown, Margaret Wise. *Wait Till the Moon is Full*. Harper & Row, 1948.

Choldenko, Gennifer. *Moonstruck*. Hyperion, 1996.

Root, Phyllis. *Moon Tiger*. Holt, 1985.

Ryder, Joanne. *The Bear on the Moon*. Morrow Junior Books, 1991.

Yolen, Jane. *Owl Moon*. Philomel, 1987.

Young, Ed. *Moon Mother*. HarperCollins, 1993.

# Two to Four-Part Plays

As you enjoy reading the poems of Jane Yolen's *Bird Watch*, discuss background, vocabulary and prior knowledge that your students may already have about birds. On chart paper, brainstorm and list as many different kinds of birds as possible. These may be as common as: chicken, duck, goose, rooster, turkey or zoo birds such as: ostrich, vulture, swan, Canadian geese, hawk, emu or as regional as: goldfinch, starling, wren, grosbeak, cowbird, chickadee and bluebird. Yolen writes her poems as she has occasion to observe the birds she describes or to have an encounter with one. After completing a list of birds, ask students to share orally any experiences they have had with one of the birds on the list. For example: Has anyone ever had a hummingbird hover near them while wearing a brightly colored shirt? Has anyone seen a bird hit a window and fall dazed or dead on the ground? Has anyone watched a bird gather sticks or string to build a nest? All of these experiences give poets and storywriters ideas for writing. After sharing their observations, direct the children in working together to create a short play. Agree to focus on a particular bird (or birds) and include two to four characters. Keep the plot simple and direct. As examples, I have included two plays that I wrote. They may give you ideas to use in creating your own class play.

## The Baby Birds

*(Two baby birds are sitting in a nest, being fed by their mother.)*

**Baby 1:**   Mmmmmm. Those worms are good, Mom.

**Baby 2:**   Hey, can I have another one?

**Baby 1:**   Where are you going, Mom?

**Mom:**   I'll be back with more, be patient. *(Mother bird flies off.)*

**Baby 1:**   Good, I'm still hungry. *(looking over the edge of the nest)* Look, I see some worms down on the ground.

**Baby 2:**   Oh, I wish we could get them.

**Baby 1:**   Well, let's fly down.

**Baby 2:**   But mom hasn't taught us how to fly yet, remember?

**Baby 1:**   Well… they sure look good.

*(The baby birds lean out so far that they fall out of the nest. They make a "tweet, tweet" noise as they flutter to the ground.)*

**Baby 2:**   Hey, we made it! Now what do we do?

**Baby 1:**   Start pulling worms.

**Baby 2:**   Wow! This is hard work. I'm getting full.

**Baby 1:**   Me, too. Let's go back home and wait for mom.

**Baby 2:**   Great idea. Shall we take a flying leap or hop, skip and jump?

**Baby 1:**   Uh-oh. We have a problem. We can't get back the same way we got down.

**Baby 2:** Start climbing.

*(The baby birds climb the tree, fall down, and climb up again. They are out of breath when they reach the nest.)*

**Baby 1:** Here comes mom with some worms.

**Mom:** Why aren't you two hungry?

**Baby 2:** We've been exercising our wings, Mom.

**Mom:** Good. Tomorrow you can fly down and get your own worms!

**Baby 1 & 2:** *(baby birds look at each other)* Oh, no!

# The Little Red Hen (Revisited)

**Narrator:** Once upon a time there was a Little Red Hen. She lived in a clean barnyard with Little Chick and Big Red Rooster. One day, Little Red Hen found straw all over her chicken coop floor.

**Little Red Hen:** Oh, my! Who will help me sweep up this straw?

**Little Chick:** Not I…

**Narrator:** …peeped Little Chick, as she waddled out to play.

**Big Red Rooster:** Not I…

**Narrator:** …cock-a-doodled Big Red Rooster as he flapped out the hen house door.

**Little Red Hen:** Then I'll do it myself…

**Narrator:** … said Little Red Hen. And she did. After the floor was swept clean, Little Red Hen noticed the dirty windows.

**Little Red Hen:** Oh, my! Who will help me wash the windows?

**Little Chick:** Not I…

**Narrator:** … peeped Little Chick, as she hurried to the grain bowl.

**Big Red Rooster:** Not I…

**Narrator:** …cock-a-doodled Big Red Rooster, as he chased after the ducks.

**Little Red Hen:** Then, I'll do it myself…

**Narrator:** … said Little Red Hen. And she did.

**Little Red Hen:** Now, who will help me dust the roosts?

**Little Chick:** Not I…

**Narrator:** … peeped Little Chick, splashing in the water dish.

**Big Red Rooster:** Not I…

**Narrator:** … cock-a-doodled Big Red Rooster, as he pecked at his breakfast corn.

**Little Red Hen:** Then, I'll do it myself…

**Narrator:** … sighed Little Red Hen. And she did. When Little Red Hen finished her work, she sat down to rest.

**Little Red Hen:** It is nearly time to fix supper. But I must take a nap first.

**Narrator:** Little Red Hen settled down in a fresh, clean nest and dozed off. Not long after, Big Red Rooster fluttered into the coop.

**Big Red Rooster:** What's for supper?…

**Narrator:** … he asked, pacing back and forth on the chicken perch.

**Little Chick:** I'm hungry…

**Narrator:** … whined Little Chick, as she bumped into Big Red Rooster. The two birds made such a fuss that they woke up Little Red Hen.

**Little Red Hen:** What's the matter? Can't you see I'm tired?

**Narrator:** Big Red Rooster scowled at Little Red Hen.

**Big Red Rooster:** My dear, why are you in such a foul mood? We're just hungry.

**Little Red Hen:** I swept up the straw. I washed the dirty windows. I dusted the roosts. And now you want me to fix supper?

**Narrator:** Little Red Hen closed her eyes, nestled back into the nest and went to sleep. Big Red Rooster looked at Little Chick and sighed.

**Big Red Rooster:** Who will help me crack the corn for supper?

**Little Chick:** Not I…

**Narrator:** … peeped Little Chick as she padded toward the door.

**Big Red Rooster:** How about going to Burger Barn, instead?…

**Narrator:** … said Big Red Rooster. And they did.

You will find that many of the stories in the book *Fables*, written by Arnold Lobel (Scholastic, 1980), can easily be adjusted into a two- to four-part play. Use a narrator (as an additional character) to explain the action, the setting and end with the story moral. Assign groups of students to work on a fable, re-writing or adjusting it to fit the number of characters you need and putting it into a play format with the character name to the extreme left of the script and the dialogue after it. Allow students to create puppets or dress up as characters to act out the fable plays. The following fables can be used to extend this activity theme of birds: "The Pelican and the Crow," "The Young Rooster," "The Bear and the Crow," "The Hen and the Apple Tree," and "The Ducks and the Fox."

---

### Additional Resources

Cresci, Maureen McCurry. *Creative Dramatics for Children.*. Scott, Foresman, 1989.

*Curtains! Familiar Plays for Little Actors.* Fearon, 1999.

*How to Do Plays With Children.* Evan-Moor 1994.

*Instructor's Big Book of Plays.* Scholastic, 1983.

Publiano, Carol. *Easy-to-read Folk and Fairy Tale Plays.* Scholastic Professional, 1997.

*Teacher's Book of Plays and Choral Readings.* Macmillan/McGraw Hill School, 1993.

---

### ★ For Younger Students

For younger students, prerecorded one- to two-part poem plays are ideal. In Jack Prelutsky's *The New Kid on the Block* (Greenwillow, 1984), you will find several poems that work as plays for one to two puppets. If you purchase Prelutsky's tape recording of selected poems from his book, students can lip sync with the poem as it's played. Otherwise, record the poem yourself on a blank cassette, using background instrumental music for a professional touch. The following Prelutsky poems from *The New Kid* work well: "I Wonder Why Dad Is so Thoroughly

Mad," "Louder than a Clap of Thunder," "When Dracula Went to the Blood Bank," "Ballad of a Boneless Chicken," "My Sister Is a Sissy," "Euphonica Jarre," "Homework! Oh, Homework!," "When Tillie Ate the Chili," and "My Dog, He Is an Ugly Dog."

Shel Silverstein's book, *Where the Sidewalk Ends* contains a few poems that can be used the same way: "Sick," "For Sale," "Warning," "Silver Fish," and "Crocodile's Toothache." Give students time to read, reread and listen to these poems so they can be memorized. It's much easier to lip sync with familiar text before putting on a puppet show. As a class, you may want to create and design the puppets that will perform these poem plays. With the help of parent volunteers, use the following puppet patterns to cut and sew the puppets in advance. Allow students to add facial features with pom-poms, moveable eyes, and yarn or fur hair. Students can create some outlandish puppet personalities that will enhance the excitement of a puppet performance. You may want to keep the finished puppets for the entire school year to use at other holiday or special celebrations.

## Making puppets

1. Enlarge the puppet patterns by 100%.
2. Place the puppet body pattern on the fold of the fabric and cut out.
3. Cut one puppet mouth on felt and one on cardboard.
4. Cut two puppet dresses.
5. Cut two puppet hands out of felt.
6. Turn the puppet body right-side out and sew the dart on the head closed.
7. Stitch from the dart to the mouth opening.
8. Stitch center front from the mouth opening to the bottom of the puppet body.
9. Making sure the dotted line edges of the felt mouth match to the corners of the mouth on the puppet head, stitch around the mouth, working the fabric carefully around the curves.
10. Turn the puppet body right-side out.
11. Fold cardboard mouth piece in half on the dotted lines to crease. Open up the cardboard mouth and spread tacky glue on. Close up cardboard mouth slightly to insert it into the puppet head. Open up the cardboard mouth piece and attach it to the inside of the felt mouth, working the cardboard to the edge of the felt mouth and smoothing out the felt.
12. Glue moveable eyes to marked area on the head. Let mouth and eyes dry. Set aside.
13. Turn puppet dress fabric wrong side out. Sew felt puppet hands to sleeve ends, then stitch all around the puppet dress. Turn puppet dress right side out.
14. For a people puppet, cut the puppet head where it's indicated on the pattern and sew the puppet head to the puppet dress.
15. Stuff the puppet head with poly-fill to keep it firm.
16. Glue yarn or fur hair to puppet head. Glue on a small pom-pom nose. Let dry.

# Puppet Patterns

Enlarge by 100%.

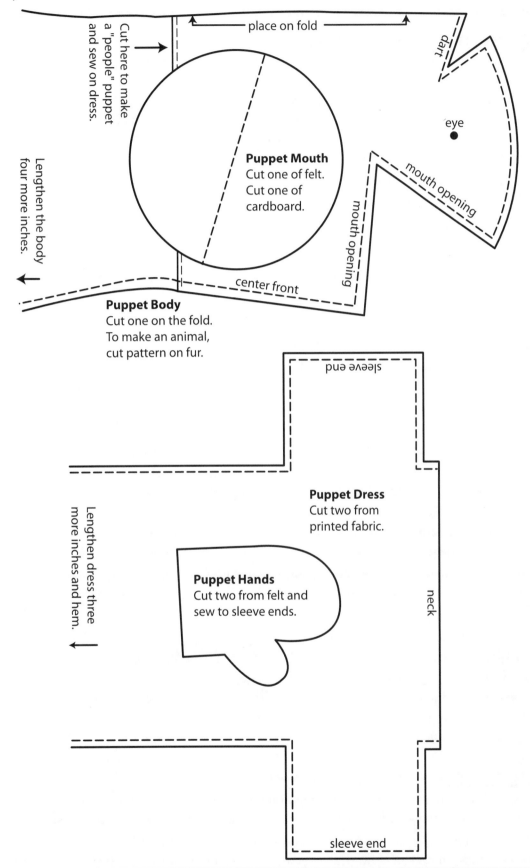

Cut here to make a "people" puppet and sew on dress.

place on fold

dart

eye

mouth opening

**Puppet Mouth**
Cut one of felt.
Cut one of cardboard.

mouth opening

Lengthen the body four more inches.

center front

**Puppet Body**
Cut one on the fold.
To make an animal,
cut pattern on fur.

sleeve end

**Puppet Dress**
Cut two from
printed fabric.

neck

Lengthen dress three more inches and hem.

**Puppet Hands**
Cut two from felt and
sew to sleeve ends.

sleeve end

# Diamonte (dee-a-MON-tay)

A diamonte is a seven-line poem shaped like a diamond. Before writing a diamonte, it helps to choose a topic and its opposite. The poem starts with one topic, then lines 5 through 7 move to a contrasting or opposite topic. Capitalize the first word of each line, separate the words with commas, then put a period at the end of the last line.

**Rules for writing a diamonte poem:**

Line 1:    a one-word topic (noun)

Line 2:    two words describing the topic (adjectives)

Line 3:    three action words (verbs)

Line 4:    four words (nouns), the first two relate to the topic of line 1, the last two relate to the topic of line 7.

Line 5:    three action words(verbs) relating to the topic of line 7

Line 6:    two words describing the topic of line 7 (adjectives)

Line 7:    one word (noun) opposite of line 1

Copy these rules on chart paper and display them in your room. Here are some sample diamonte poems to share with your class:

Teacher
Adult, patient
Helping, teaching, motivating
Math, reading, art, music
Drawing, singing, creating
Curious, learner
Student.

Summer
Hot, busy, fun
Swimming, fishing, hiking
Bicycle, trampoline, snowmobile, sled
Sliding, skating, ice-fishing
Cold, snowy
Winter.

Some students may need further encouragement to write diamontes. Try supplying some of the words and leaving blanks for students to fill in. Here are some samples:

City
Crowded, _____
Beeping, pushing, _____
Skyscrapers, _____, tractors, _____
Planting, harvesting, _____
Quiet, _____
Country.

Christmas
Happy, _____
Baking, decorating, _____
Tree, _____, basket, _____
Hunting, hopping, _____
Spring, _____
Easter.

## ★ For Older Students

Have older students choose their two contrasting words, follow the rules and allow them time to create their diamonte poem. The following are some opposites or contrasting topic ideas:

king – queen, seed – plant, autumn – spring, birth – death, egg – bird, earthquake – hurricane, giant – dwarf, sun – rain, joy – sadness, sickness – health

 Activity Six

# Holiday Games

Jane Yolen's *The Three Bears Holiday Rhyme Book* includes fifteen poems depicting various holidays throughout the year and how they might be celebrated by Goldilocks and the Three Bears. Before reading Yolen's holiday poem book you may wish to acquaint your students with "The Three Bears" by rereading or retelling it, depending on your grade level. The colorful illustrations will delight your children as you read the poems to coincide with upcoming holidays. Couple this book with Jane Yolen's *The Three Bears* and you'll have a wonderful start to a bear theme.

---

**Additional Resources:**

Blocksma, Mary. *The Best Dressed Bear.* Children's Press, 1984.

Degen, Bruce. *Jamberry.* Harper Trophy, 1983.

Douglas, Barbara. *Good As New.* Mulberry, 1982.

Freeman, Don. *Corduroy.* Viking, 1978.

Hofmann, Ginnie. *Who Wants an Old Teddy Bear?* Random House, 1978.

Minarik, Else Holmelund. *Little Bear's Visit.* Harper Trophy, 1979.

---

## Games

Children of all ages enjoy playing games, especially if there is a little competitive edge and challenge to them. For younger students, the practice of orally counting spaces and matching one-to-one as they follow the game board path is a precursor to tracking words on the printed page. Whether it's to develop pre-reading skills or provide reading practice, extend students holiday enjoyment by creating games that will amuse and entertain as well. Over the years I've created games for each holiday and season of the school year, which roughly adds up to one to two games a month.

To make holiday games get help from your students, parent volunteers, or room parents in collecting and cutting out magazine, calendar or bulletin board pictures appropriate for the holiday. You may wish to start a picture file on each holiday in advance to be prepared for upcoming projects.

### Halloween Game

**To prepare**

You will need poster paper approximately 22" x 28". Cut out a large magazine or calendar picture of a jack-o'-lantern and glue it in the upper left corner of the poster paper. Write the word "Start" above the picture. Cut out a magazine picture of a black cat, glue it in the bottom right corner of the poster paper and write the word "Finish" below the picture. In the blank area at the top of the poster, title your game board "The H-O-W-L-oween Game." Duplicate and cut the following pictures, gluing them end-to-end and side-by-side, to make a pathway from the "Start" picture (top left corner) to the "Finish" picture (bottom right corner).

---

**Pathway Pictures**

**Sample Gameboard**

Outline a boxed area for the penalty card deck to be placed on the game board. Randomly color five of the pathway pictures. When students land on these during the game, they need to draw a penalty card, read it aloud and do what it says. Color in some boxes on the pathway to indicate a shortcut trail from one side of the pathway to the other. Place arrows to indicate the direction players would move on the shortcut. When students roll the die and end their count on the shortcut square, they are to follow the arrows and slide to the end square of the shortcut and stop.

Use Halloween stickers or pictures to decorate the game board between the pathway areas. To make the penalty cards, cut blank 3" x 5" index cards in half.

**Copy the following sentences, one on each penalty card:**

1. Go ahead to the nearest pumpkin.
2. Go ahead to the nearest owl.
3. Go ahead to the nearest cat.
4. Go ahead to the nearest witch.
5. Go ahead to the nearest skeleton.
6. Go ahead to the nearest spider web.
7. Go ahead to the nearest ghost.
8. Go ahead to the nearest spider.
9. You dropped your flashlight in a mud puddle. Go back 5 spaces.
10. Trade places with another player.
11. You scared your teacher. Go back 2 spaces.
12. You ate too much candy and got sick. Go back to start.
13. You lost your Halloween mask. Lose one turn.
14. Someone stole your jack-o'-lantern and you feel bad. Go back 4 spaces.
15. Take an extra turn.
16. You cut your finger when you carved your pumpkin. Go back 1 space.
17. Your costume scared your baby brother. Go back 2 spaces.
18. You dropped your candy all over the sidewalk. Go back 3 spaces.
19. You shared your candy with your sister. Go ahead 4 spaces.
20. You won a prize for your costume. Go to finish.
21. You saw a ghost on Halloween night. Go back 4 spaces.
22. You dressed up as a scarecrow for Halloween. Go ahead 2 spaces.
23. Make a noise like a ghost and move ahead 10 spaces.
24. Go to the shortcut space and slide.
25. You went trick-or-treating in the pouring rain. Go back 1 space.

Laminate the game board and cards for durability.

### How to play

All players place their game markers on the "start" pumpkin. Place the penalty card deck face down in the boxed-in area on the game board. Each player gets a turn to roll the die. The highest number determines the player who will begin the game. Play proceeds in a clockwise direction. The first player rolls the die and moves that number of spaces. If a player lands on a colored picture, he/she draws a penalty card, reads it and does what it says. The player places the penalty card face down under the penalty card deck and play continues to the next player. If a player lands on the shortcut square, he/she follows the arrows to the last square and stops. Play continues until the exact number is rolled to get to the finish.

## Happy New Year! Game

### To prepare

This game is played during the month of January to teach and review calendar facts. You will need a 22"x 28" piece of colored poster paper. Decorate and cut out large construction paper party hats to use as the "Start" and "Finish" area. Glue the "Start" party hat at the top left corner of the poster paper, and the "Finish" party hat to the bottom right of the poster paper. Using a black marker, write "Start" and "Finish" on the party hats. To make the pathway from start to finish, duplicate the following party hat patterns on white paper and cut out.

Arrange the party hats on the gameboard first, then glue in place. Randomly color five to seven of the party hats to indicate players will draw a "calendar fact card" and answer it. To make the fact card deck, cut 3"x 5" cards in half. Outline a boxed-in area for the fact card deck to be placed on the gameboard. Decorate the gameboard with balloons, confetti, stickers, etc., then laminate. Have a new year (January) calendar available for students to use while playing the game.

### Write the following questions, one on each fact card:

1. What holiday comes in January? (New Year's Day)
2. Without looking, how do you spell the name of this month? (J-a-n-u-a-r-y)
3. What is the last month of the year? (December)
4. On which day of the week did January begin? (check calendar)
5. How many days are in January? (31)
6. Which day of the week does New Year's Day fall on?
7. What month comes after January? (February)
8. What year is this?
9. What day was it yesterday?
10. What season is the month of January in? (Winter)
11. What is next Thursday's date?
12. How many months are left in this year?
13. What is today's date?
14. How many months are in a year? (12)
15. How many days are left in January?
16. What day does the 27th fall on?
17. On which day of the week will January end?
18. What is the abbreviation for January? (Jan.)
19. What month comes before January?
20. What are the dates of all the Saturdays in January?
21. Take another turn!
22. Lose a turn!
23. Go ahead 3 spaces!
24. Go back 3 spaces!
25. Go to Finish!

 **How to play**

All players place their game markers on the "Start" party hat. Each player gets a turn to roll the die. The highest number determines the player who will begin the game. Play proceeds in a clockwise direction. The first player rolls the die and moves that number of spaces on the gameboard. If the player lands on a colored party hat, he picks a "calendar fact card," reads it aloud, answers it or does what it says. If the player gets a fact question, they may use the January calendar to help answer it. If they answer correctly they move ahead one space. If they cannot, they move back one, but share the correct answer before going on. Play continues until the exact number is rolled to reach the "Finish" space.

## "Have a Heart" Valentine Game

### To prepare

You will need a 22" x 28" piece of poster paper. Cut out two large, red construction paper hearts. In black marker, write "Start" on one heart and "Finish" on the other. Glue the "Start" heart at the top left corner of the poster paper, and the "Finish" heart at the bottom right corner. To make your Valentine pathway, vary the sizes of your construction paper hearts, using the colors red, white, lavender and pink. Decorate your gameboard with new or recycled Valentine cards and stickers. For larger decorations, use calendar, magazine or bulletin board pictures you can purchase at grocery or department stores around that time of year. Decorate five to seven of the Valentine pathway hearts in a special (fancy) way to indicate that players will draw a card when they land on these fancy hearts. Simply cut a different colored, smaller heart and glue it in the middle of the pathway heart to make it stand out. Number the fancy hearts.

Outline a boxed-in area on the gameboard to place your "draw-a-card" deck. To make the "draw-a-card" set of cards, cut 3" x 5" cards in half .

### Write the following sentences, one on each card:

1.  You brought a treat for your class party. Go ahead 4 spaces.
2.  Your Valentine mailbox split apart. Go back 1 space.
3.  You lost your candy on the way to school. Lose 1 turn.
4.  You got sick from eating all of your candy. Go back 5 spaces.
5.  You gave the principal a Valentine card. Go ahead 4 spaces.
6.  You won the Valentine's Day game. Go ahead 10 spaces.
7.  You lost your friend's Valentine card. Go back 2 spaces.
8.  You gave all your friends a Valentine pencil. Go ahead 3 spaces.
9.  Your Valentine mailbox is full of cards. Go to fancy heart number 5.
10. You tripped and spilled juice all over your friend's face at the Valentine's party. Go back 5 spaces.
11. You gave your teacher a Valentine hug. Take another turn.
12. Your dog ate your Valentine candy. Go back 2 spaces.
13. Red is your favorite color. Go ahead 6 spaces.
14. Switch spaces with another player.

15. You dropped your Valentine cards in the mud. Go back 3 spaces.

16. You baked a cake for your mother on Valentine's Day. Go ahead 3 spaces.

17. You left your Valentine cards at home. Go back 4 spaces.

18. You cut your tongue when you licked the Valentine card envelopes. Go to fancy heart number 1.

19. You took a Valentine heart to a sick friend. Take another turn.

20. You may go to the "Finish" heart.

21. Go to fancy heart number 2.

22. Go to fancy heart number 3.

23. Go to fancy heart number 4.

24. Go to fancy heart number 5.

25. Go to fancy heart number 6.

## How to play

All players place their game markers on the "Start" heart. Each player gets a turn to roll the die. The highest number determines the player who will begin the game. Play proceeds in a clockwise direction. The first player rolls the die and moves that number of spaces on the game board. If the player lands on a "fancy" heart, she picks from the "draw-a-card" pile. The player reads the card aloud and does as it says. The player places the card face down under the "draw-a-card" deck. Play continues until the exact number is rolled to reach the "Finish" space.

## Poet Tree

To poetically enhance each holiday, season or monthly theme, purchase an artificial tree for your classroom. Place this tree in a corner of your room and label the planter pot, "Poet Tree." Starting in September, cut out apple shapes from red construction paper, add a brown stem and green leaf, then stick a white label on the apple cutout. Copy a variety of short poems, one on each apple. Laminate. Hole punch the leaf of the apple, insert a Christmas tree ornament hook (or open up a paper clip), and hang the apples all over the tree. This is a good way to start off the school year by making poetry an important part of your classroom. Each morning choose one or two students to pick an apple off the tree and read the poem-of-the-day. Place the monthly title, "Apple-tizing Poems" on a laminated strip above or near the "Poet Tree." Enlarge and duplicate the following monthly patterns:

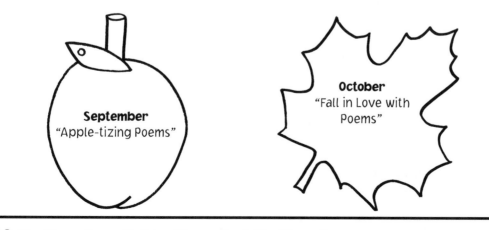

September
"Apple-tizing Poems"

October
"Fall in Love with Poems"

**November**
"Poem-kin Pie"

**December**
"Tree-mendous Poems"

**January**
"Sno-emflakes"

**February**
"Poetry from the Heart"

**April**
"Spring into Poetry"

**March**
"St. Patty's Poems"

**May**
"Petal Poems"

**June**
"Drift Away with Poems"

 Activity Seven

# Tanka

Tanka is a form of unrhymed Japanese poem often written about the seasons of the year or nature. It consists of five lines with a syllable pattern of 5-7-5-7-7. Tanka poems have 31 syllables in all. For example:

### Mother's Day

(5) Who cradled and sang

(7) So late in the quiet night?

(5) Who showed me the love

(7) I will no never forget?

(7) My Mother, dear Mother, you.

### Valentine's Day

(5) I bought this lace card

(7) It's especially for you.

(5) I signed and sealed it

(7) A secret message to you.

(7) I'll always love you daddy!

Assist students on how to begin writing tankas. Give them support as you work together on filling in the following missing lines (suggestions added):

### Spring

(5) Little ladybugs

(7) Flitting on the window panes

(5) Are you lost or sad?

(7) I'll take you outside today

(7) (To find your black-dotted friends).

### Fall

(5) The leaves are flying

(7) Every which way and that.

(5) The wind is swirling

(7) In a leafy tornado

(7) (Catch them, rake them, hold them down.)

As students feel more comfortable with this poem form, allow them to create tankas on their own. Give them opportunities to brainstorm words and phrases first, then remind them about the 5-7-5-7-7 syllable pattern. Use the following support by writing it on chart paper and brainstorming together or making it a worksheet exercise:

1.   List some words and phrases that make you think of summer:

_____       _____

_____       _____

_____       _____

_____       _____

_____       _____

Now use your words and phrases to write a tanka about summer. Remember to use the
5-7-5-7-7 syllable pattern:

_____

_____

_____

_____

_____

2.   List some words and phrases that make you think of winter:

_____   _____

_____   _____

_____   _____

Now use your words and phrases to write a tanka about winter. Remember to use the
5-7-5-7-7 syllable pattern:

_____

_____

_____

_____

_____

(Suggestions for words and phrases about summer: hot weather, long days, fun with
friends, camping, swimming. Suggestions for words and phrases about winter: icicles, skiing,
snowmobiling, very cold weather, Christmas, cozy and warm inside.)

 Activity Eight

# Acrostics

Jane Yolen's *Best Witches* contains Halloween poems of different kinds. She uses riddles,
jump rope rhymes, word plays, a friendly letter and unrhymed poetry. Several of her poem
titles could easily be turned into acrostic poems using details from the poem itself. Try using
other holidays or seasons as acrostic titles as well. Acrostic poems are fun to write. The first
letter of each line will spell out the topic of the poem. Acrostics do not need to rhyme.

**How to get started**

1.   Choose a topic word. It could be a name of a person, place or thing.

2.   Write the letters of the word down the page in large print.

3.   Make up phrases that begin with each letter of your acrostic topic.

You may wish to have a dictionary and thesaurus available to aid students in choosing words. Start out short and simple by using topics like: frogs, trees, and flag. Ask students to brainstorm phrases that would tell facts or fiction about the topic.

### Suggestions

**F** orever hopping in my garden

"**R** ibbit, ribbit" is his song while

**O** vereating flies and mosquitoes. They are

**G** reen and

**S** limy.

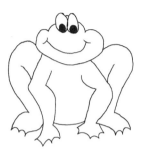

Students may wish to write an acrostic poem about their hometown or the state they live in. For example:

**N** ever want to leave the country

**E** very day is an adventure

**W** inding paths and secret trails

**Y** ou can go fishing,

**O** r canoeing, hiking or

**R** ock climbing. I just want to

**K** eep the smell of country air.

### "Getting-to-know-you"

As a back to school activity, ask students to make a personal acrostic using their name. This is a great way to introduce themselves to their classmates. Here are some samples:

**P** izza is my favorite food

**A** lways athletic

**U** se a computer for everything

**L** eft-handed.

**C** ares about animals

**I** s shy

**N** ever has a messy bedroom

**D** ogs are my favorite pet

**Y** ellow is my favorite color.

Students may want to add an illustration to their acrostic as well. Display these acrostic poems on a "Getting-to-know-you" bulletin board for students to read throughout the day. This activity makes a great display for your school's open house as well as an addition to student portfolios.

# Vocabulary Development

Jane Yolen's *Dinosaur Dances* is an incredible book featuring dinosaurs dancing to different types of music and the whole dance floor scene. The whimsical illustrations and bright colors capture your attention immediately! Students of every age share a common interest and curiosity about these extinct creatures. Spend several days reading all the poems in this book with your students. Capitalize on the discussion and comments that will be generated from this theme. Then you may want to share the following poem I did on dinosaurs with them:

### Dinosaurs Could 'a

Dinosaurs could 'a been red or green.
They could 'a been kind and never mean.
Dinosaurs could 'a been checkered brown.
They could 'a worn ties and vests to town.

Dinosaurs could 'a been striped or spotted.
They could 'a been blue and white polka-dotted.
Dinosaurs could 'a loved snow and rain.
They could 'a been smart with their tiny pea brain.

Dinosaurs could 'a been talented dancers.
They could 'a been disco-ers, waltzers and prancers.
Dinosaurs could 'a blushed and winked.
But we'll never know, 'cause now they're extinct.

## V.I.X. Games

Using words from a variety of these poems, create a "V.I.X. Game," or Vocabulary Improvement Experience game. Students will categorize 30 vocabulary words under three topics. For V.I.X. #1 the topics are "clothing," "dances," and "at a party." To make this game, cut fifteen 3"x 5" cards (for small groups) in half lengthwise. Use 5"x 8" cards for large groups. Write the following words on the card halves:

**Clothing words:**

frock, tuxedo, smock, suit, sari, formal, suspenders, loincloth, bellbottoms, overalls

**Dance words:**

disco, waltz, jig, polka, square, samba, jitterbug, twist, tango, ballroom

**"At a party" words:**

celebrate, grill, roast, presents, prize, games, marshmallows, lotion, citronella, patio

Using a black marker, write the topics on colored construction paper strips. Laminate all cards and place a magnetic strip on the back of each.

## How to play

Place the topic strips in a row on a magnetic board or chalkboard. Mix up all the word cards and pass out one word card per child (for a small group, pass out two or more cards). Ask students, three at a time, to go to the board and place their word cards under the right topic. After all the words are categorized, discuss each column by repeating the word and checking to see if it is in the correct column. If not, change it. If students are unsure of the word definitions, get out a dictionary and give different students opportunities to look up the words in question. Using *Dinosaur Dances* and other books, show students pictures that illustrate the various vocabulary words from the lists. Some students, because of their experience or background knowledge may be able to demonstrate or describe the meanings of the words, hence the name of the game Vocabulary Improvement Experience. As the teacher, be prepared to demonstrate as well or have someone available to show students some of the dance steps, if interested. In this way, all students will benefit and broaden their vocabulary base. When finished with this activity, store all the cards in a 9"x 12", string-tied manila envelope. Label the envelope V.I.X. #1. Here are some suggestions for more V.I.X. activities:

## V.I.X #2

**Feelings:**

 terrible, cheery, sleepy, eager, grateful, sorrowful, bashful, glad, bad, satisfied

**Appearance:**

 beautiful, handsome, broad, sagging, ragged, disguised, neat, huge, stiff, cute

**Ways to move:**

 rapidly, gracefully, quietly, backwards, lively, whirl, twirl, dodge, glide, wobble

## V.I.X. #3

**Footwear:**

 sandals, slippers, loafers, oxfords, moccasins, boots, shoes, roller skates, galoshes

**Sweet things:**

 chocolate, mints, ice cream, doughnuts, sundae, applesauce, gingerbread, pudding, licorice

**About water:**

 shallow, muddy, bubbles, suds, bath, leak, shower, slush, pour

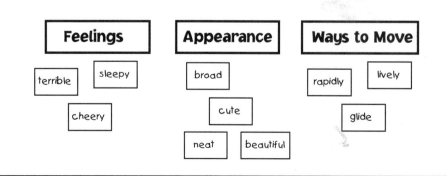

 Activity Ten

# Cinquain

A cinquain (sin-KANE) is a five-line, unrhymed poem. Each line follows a specific pattern. Here are the rules:

Line 1 – 1 word, a noun (usually the title)

Line 2 – 2 words, adjectives (describing line one)

Line 3 – 3 words, action verbs

Line 4 – 4 words, expressing feeling about the topic

Line 5 – 1 word, a synonym for line 1 (topic)

Read students some examples of cinquains. You may want to pre-write the rules and examples on poster paper for students to use as a guide when they begin to practice writing them.

**Examples:**

| | |
|---|---|
| Bubblegum | Hummingbird |
| Ooey, gooey | Tiny, colorful |
| Smacking, chewing, blowing, | Flitting, fluttering, speeding |
| Delicious bubbles of sweetness | Please hold still once |
| Bazooka. | Hummer. |

Assist students in writing cinquains by providing some of the words. Put these sample fill-in cinquains on large poster paper and brainstorm words as a class or put them on a hand-out sheet for students to experiment independently. Allow students time to share these orally.

| | |
|---|---|
| Sun | Homework |
| _____, _____ | _____, _____ |
| Warming, tanning, _____ | Reading, _____, _____ |
| _____ _____ _____ summertime | _____ _____ _____ _____ |
| Fireball. | Brainwork. |

Brainstorm a list of words to which students can refer. The students who would like to continue on can do so independently. Examples: pool, birthday, caterpillar, popsicle, bathtub, iguana, tennis, garbage, ostrich, taco, bicycle, hamster, school, tractor, farm, rose, fire, treasure, moon, baby.

# Birthday Celebrations

Jane Yolen's book titled *Mouse's Birthday* is a sing-songy way to start a birthday celebration in your classroom. Students will enjoy the repetition and rhyme as Mouse's friends come with a birthday gift and try to fit into Mouse's very small house. To make your student birthdays a special event, decorate a bulletin board and make it into an activity center. Trim and staple a plain, plastic, brightly colored tablecloth to fit your bulletin board. Using a fancy stencil, cut letters to make the words "Happy Birthday to You," and place the words at the top of the bulletin board. Decorate the outside edge of the bulletin board with small, blown-up balloons stapled in place. Enlarge, color, and cut out a picture of a decorated birthday cake to place in the middle of the birthday bulletin board. All around the birthday cake, place colored construction paper musical notes labeled with student names and birth dates. At the birthday activity center, display several birthday theme books for the birthday student to read, browse and enjoy throughout the day.

Provide birthday-themed stationery or creative scrapbooking pages (found at craft supply stores) and pencils for the birthday student to write about a family "Birthday Memory." Ask student to leave their writing piece at the birthday activity center for other students to read throughout the day. As a special touch, take a photo of the birthday student standing in front of the bulletin board. Keep the photo and place it in your own classroom photo album along with the child's "Birthday Memory" writing piece. At the end of the school year, allow each student to take their photo and writing home. For summer birthday students, you may wish to schedule their birthday celebration at an appropriate time during the school year, rather than the very last month of school.

To add a little variety, sing a different birthday song. Try these words to the tune of "Pop Goes the Weasel."

### Birthday Song

Today we have a birthday boy (girl)

So pat the person's shoulder.

Have a happy birthday, _____ (child's name)!

Now you're one year older.

---

## Resources for a Birthday Activity Center

Asch, Frank. *Happy Birthday Moon*. Prentice-Hall, 1982.

Bender, Robert. *The Preposterous Rhinoceros*. Henry Holt, 1994.

Brown, Marc. *Arthur's Birthday*. Little, Brown, 1989.

Cameron, Ann. *Julian, Dream Doctor*. Random House, 1990.

Carle, Eric. *The Secret Birthday Message*. HarperTrophy, 1986.

Clewes, Dorothy. *The Birthday*. Coward-McCann, 1963.

Delaney, Molly. *Birthday Blizzard*. Morrow Junior, 1993.

Eisenberg, Lisa. *Happy Birthday, Lexie!* Viking, 1991.

Giff, Patricia Reilly. *Happy Birthday, Ronald Morgan!* Viking Kestrel, 1986.

Green, John. *Alice and the Birthday Giant*. Scholastic, 1989.

Hest, Amy. *Jamaica Louise James*. Candlewick Press, 1996.

Jonas, Ann. *The 13th Clue*. Greenwillow Books, 1992.

Mayer, Mercer. *Bun Bun's Birthday*. Random House, 1983.

Modell, Frank. *Ice Cream Soup*. Greenwillow Books, 1988.

Munsch, Robert. *Moira's Birthday*. Annick Press, 1987.

Patz, Nancy. *No Thumpin', No Bumpin', No Rumpus Tonight!* Atheneum, 1990.

Polacco, Patricia. *Some Birthday!* Simon & Schuster, 1991.

Prager, Annabelle. *The Surprise Party*. Pantheon Books, 1977.

Yolen, Jane. *Picnic with Piggins*. Harcourt Brace Jovanovich, 1988.

## Extending the Mouse Theme

To extend the "mouse" theme consider reading *If You Give a Mouse a Cookie* by Laura Joffe Numeroff (Scholastic, 1985). Children love this "round-about" story of a mouse going from one messy activity to another, which ends with another cookie for him. Share Numeroff's other two books titled, *If You Give a Pig a Pancake* (HarperCollins, 1998) and *If You Give a Moose a Muffin* (Scholastic, 1991).

Discuss the words and format of a "round-about" story pattern that Numeroff uses. Brainstorm and list on chart paper, some similar story titles so that the whole class could create a story which follows the "round-about" story pattern. For instance: *If You Give a Duck a Donut*, *If You Give a Cow a Cupcake*, *If you give a Snake Some Soup*, etc. Record students' ideas as they brainstorm crazy situations, places and trouble the character gets into and how to end the story. Use the three picture books as a guide in rewriting and editing your story. Keep the finished story chart visible for students to re-read and enjoy.

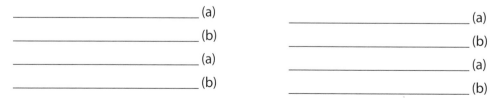

# Quatrains and Clerihew

A quatrain is a four-line poem that rhymes. Quatrains may have different rhyme schemes. This means that each ending rhyme sound is given a letter of the alphabet, this first line is designated with an (a). Each time that same end rhyme sound appears in the poem, it has the same letter. A new ending rhyme sound would be given another letter, the second is (b). The most common rhyme schemes found in quatrains are "aabb" and "abcb." Notice the rhyme schemes of the following quatrains.

Snow is coming down sooooo hard. (a)
Wish I could play in the yard. (a)
But Mom's afraid of one silly thing... (b)
She might not find me 'til next spring! (b)

My mother goes to ballet. (a)
She's in the class with me. (b)
I wear a ruffled, pink tutu. (c)
Mom wears a white three-three. (b)

Spring is here, I know becuz (a)
The attic flies are all a buzz. (a)
Windows are full of buzzling flecks, (b)
Leaving behind those nasty specks. (b)

Country air is clean and fresh, (a)
Much healthier, for sure. (b)
Unless the farmer up the road (c)
Decides to spread manure. (b)

As students try writing quatrains, assist them by providing some rhyming words:

_____ mouse (a)
_____ house (a)
_____ fright (b)
_____ night (b)

_____ garbage (a)
_____ junk (b)
_____ neighbors (c)
_____ stunk (b)

Try some different rhyme schemes for fun:

_____ (a)          _____ (a)
_____ (b)          _____ (b)
_____ (a)          _____ (a)
_____ (b)          _____ (b)

Here are some topics to write about: my favorite sport, our vacation, grandma's house, my pet, Halloween night, my big brother, our brand new pool, winter's coming, a birthday surprise, sick with the flu.

## Clerihew

A clerihew (KLER-e-hyoo) is a four-line poem or quatrain. The first two lines rhyme together and the last two lines rhyme together. The rhyme scheme must follow the aabb pattern. A clerihew tells something about a person in a humorous way. The person's name must be the last word in the first line. A person's name may be difficult to rhyme. It's helpful to think of several rhyming words first before you begin to write. If a name has more than one syllable, find a rhyming word for the last syllable only as in these examples I created:

I love to read Dr. Seuss.
If you don't have books, there's no excuse.
Visit your library, go to the store,
There you'll find books galore.

I've seen my favorite, Mickey Mouse
On Saturday cartoons at my house.
But Disney World is where I'd go
To see Mickey in a real live show.

Assist students with this poem activity by first brainstorming a list of famous or well-known people. Write the names on the chalkboard or chart paper. The following are suggestions: Bob Hope, Henry Ford, Princess Di, Tom Cruise, Babe Ruth, Pocahontas, Christopher Columbus, Walt Disney, Einstein, Daniel Boone, Betsy Ross, George Washington, Cher, George Burns, Squanto, Abe Lincoln, Martin Luther King Jr, Tim Allen, Garth Brooks, Barbara Walters, Big Foot.

Pick two or three names from above. List rhyming words to go with each name to demonstrate the next step to writing a clerihew. For example:

| **Martin Luther King** | **Babe Ruth** | **Garth Brooks** |
|---|---|---|
| sing, bring, ring, fling | truth, booth, youth, tooth | hooks, cooks, books, nooks, |

Now, give students an opportunity to write a clerihew from the rhyming word examples above or come up with their own ideas.

_____ (a)
_____ (a)
_____ (b)
_____ (b)

Challenge your students to write a clerihew about someone they know personally—*themselves*!

_____ (a)
_____ (a)
_____ (b)
_____ (b)

# Creative Expression and Following Directions

After reading Jane Yolen's book titled *Water Music* you may be motivated to purchase a camera and try filming some unique water displays of your own to write about. Create an opportunity to challenge your students to capture nature on film and write about it. Plan a class photography/writing contest around the theme of "water."

Poll your students to find out how many of them own cameras or have access to a camera. Consider approaching your school parent group to purchase inexpensive or disposable cameras for this class contest. You may want to set aside some time during the day to assist students in planning and brainstorming ideas for photos. If your school is situated near or around water, then a nature walk may be appropriate. You may want to invite a photographer or experienced parent to come and share some simple rules and tips of photography with your class. Be sure to take extra water photos yourself to have available for special circumstances. Using chart paper, brainstorm and write a list of ideas on possible "water" pictures students could photograph, such as: a dripping faucet, water in a tiny stream, water sprinkler on the lawn, mud puddle, pond ripples after throwing a stone in, sweat pouring off your face, dog lapping up water, rain coming off the roof or gutter, windshield wipers on a rainy day, drinking fountain, splashing water in a pool, birds in a bird bath, watering a flower garden, squirt gun fight, washing dishes, mopping the floor, washing your hair, water fountain, fish jumping out of a stream, men fishing. Post the following contest rules for your students to read carefully (following directions):

## Photography/Writing Contest

### Rules

1. The photography/writing contest entries are due no later than _____ (date).

2. Submit your poem (rhymed or unrhymed) on an 8"x 11" sheet of white paper with your name in the top left corner.

3. Write your name on the back of your photo and place it on top of your poem sheet.

4. Place all entries in the contest box on your teacher's desk.

5. Contest winners will be announced _____ (date). The winning entries will be sent to our local newspaper for publication. All entries will be displayed in our classroom book titled *Reflections on Water*.

At the end of the school year, consider getting colored copies of the album pages to keep as samples for the following year. Allow students to take their originals home and share them with their family.

# Poetry Learning Station

Another whole class activity is to create a poetry learning station in your classroom. You will need a comfortable-sized area as well as a large supply of poetry books. Set the books on shelves, tables, desks, magazine racks, dividers, or an overhead wire display, for easy access. Post a decorative, eye-appealing "Poetry Center Assignment" sheet or poster at the learning station so students can follow specific directions to complete their tasks. Supply a file folder for each student to place their work in. Store the files in a colorful file crate or box at the poetry station. Be sure to introduce and acquaint students with the directions, materials, supplies, and books at the center before they proceed independently. Advance preparation is necessary to create task or job cards for students to select, read through and complete.

The following is a list of materials you will need to make the poetry learning station task cards:

| | |
|---|---|
| scissors, glue, markers | clear and printed contact paper |
| white/colored, unruled 4"x6" cards | bulletin board decorations |
| 8 ½" x 11" white and colored paper | scrapbooking pages |
| a variety of pictures from magazines | stickers, seasonal punch-out pictures |
| old calendars and used greeting cards | boxes or envelops for the task cards |
| old phonics or language workbooks | |

## Time of the Year Task Cards

Construct a set of "Time-of-the-Year" task cards from 8½"x11" paper. Decorate a page for each holiday, season or theme of the year: back-to-school, Yom Kippur, fall, Rosh Hashanah, Columbus Day, Halloween, winter, Veteran's Day, Thanksgiving, Christmas, Hanukkah, snow, New Year's Day, Martin Luther King Jr. Day, President's Day, Valentine's Day, rain, spring, St. Patrick's Day, Easter, Mother's Day, Memorial Day, Flag Day, summer, Independence Day (July 4th), Labor Day. For consistency and organizational purposes, label the top of each decorated task card page with the title and the holiday, season or theme. For example a fall card is shown here.

**25  Time of the Year: Fall**

Find a poem about fall or write one of your own.

**Time-of-the-Year Card**

Place a number in the top left corner of each task card page, from 1 to 25. At the bottom of each task card, write the following directions: <u>Find</u> a poem about "fall" or <u>write</u> one of your own. (Substitute the other holiday, season or theme words in the parenthesis for each task card page). Laminate the task cards for durability.

Students then, look for or write a poem about "fall" and copy it on the record sheet that has been duplicated and placed in the box along with the Time-of-the-Year task cards.

Decorate a box with the printed contact paper, to store the 8½"x 11" task cards. Use a black marker to write the title, "Time-of-the-Year" on a white 3" x 5" card. Secure the index card (with a small piece of tape) to the cover of the contact papered box. Then place a larger piece of clear contact paper over the entire title card and press in place. This labeled box will identify and protect the task cards for future use.

**Time of the Year Record Sheet**

Name: _____

Date: _____

Holiday, Season or theme:
_____

Card Number: _____

Poem:

**Record Sheet**

## Animal Antics Task Cards

Construct a set of "Animal" task cards for your poetry learning station. Using a variety of animal pictures, depicting animals in action or humorous poses, decorate several 8½"x 11" (or change the size for variety) pages for this set of task cards. You may want to find pictures of the following animals to cut out and glue onto the task cards: (wild animals) zebra, elephant, giraffe, hippopotamus, alligator, gorilla, rhinoceros, panda bear, lion, ostrich, penguin, anteater, sloth, (pets) dog, cat, hamster, rabbit, gerbil, iguana, snake, etc. Title each task card, "Animal Antics," and place a number in the top left corner (30+). Write the following directions at the bottom of each task card: Find a poem about this animal or write one of your own. Laminate the task cards. Students will copy or write an animal poem on the record sheet that is to be duplicated and placed in the box along with the task cards.

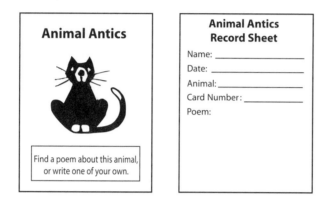

## Picture Poetry Task Cards

For students who enjoy drawing, give them an opportunity to illustrate poems in this next set of poetry task cards. Construct "Picture-Poetry" cards from 8½"x 11" paper. Use a variety of short poems that will clearly inspire students to create an illustration. Write a short poem on each task card with a small visual (of the theme or topic) of the poem. For example:

### a Dog's Life
**Anonymous**

I had a dog, his name was Rover.
When he rolled, he rolled in clover!
When he died, he died all over.
Goodbye, Rover.

*Glue a picture of a dog on the task card, so students can get a visual "jump start" before creating their illustration.*

### There Was a Young Farmer
**Anonymous**

There was a young farmer of Leeds
Who swallowed six packets of seeds.
It soon came to pass
He was covered with grass,
And he couldn't sit down for the weeds.

*Cut out and glue the front portion of six seed packets to the task cards as a "starter" visual.*

## The Hazards of Science

**(Anonymous)**

A green little chemist
On a green little day
Mixed some green little chemicals
In a green little way.

The green little grasses
Now tenderly wave
O'er the green little chemist's
Green little grave.

*Find a picture of a man in a lab coat from a science or medical magazine to create a visual image for students to continue with.*

---

### Picture Poetry Record Sheet

Name: _____

Date: _____

Name of poem: _____

Card number: _____

Picture:

---

For more picture-poetry ideas, check various anthologies for poems which do not have illustrations. *Where the Sidewalk Ends* by Shel Silverstein, has some picture perfect possibilities, such as: "Magic," "Colors," "Smart," "Rain," "Ridiculous Rose," "Thumbs," "Point of View," "Eighteen Flavors," "Instructions," and "Standing." To complete this set of task cards, label the top of each card. "Picture-Poetry," and place a number in the top left corner (50+). Copy the picture-poem in the top half of the card, then cut and glue on a "starter" visual. At the bottom of each task card write the following directions: "Create an illustration to go with this poem." Students will make their drawing on the record sheet that has been duplicated and placed in the box along with the picture-poetry task cards. Laminate the task cards. Prepare a box or envelop to attractively store your task cards at the poetry learning station.

## Poetivity Task Cards

The final set of task cards for your station are "Poetivity" cards (poetry activity cards) that will be made with colored 4"x 6" unruled index cards, and various small pictures or stickers to decorate with. You need to title each 4"x 6" task card, "Poetivity #1," "Poetivity #2," and so on. Write the following ideas on your poetivity task cards:

1. Find or write a poem about your favorite sport. (Cut and glue on a small picture of children playing baseball, soccer, etc.)

2. Find or write a poem about a special friend. (Cut and glue on a picture of a dog, cat, or person with a child.)

3. Find or write a poem about "fishing." (Cut and glue on a picture of someone fishing.)

4. Find or write a poem about "safety." (Cut and glue on a picture of a stop sign, etc.)

5. Find or write a poem about "good health." (Cut and glue on a picture of vegetables, grooming, etc.)

6. Find and copy several poems about birds. Make a bird poem book.

7. Find and copy several poems about cats. Make a cat-shaped poem book.

8. Write a poem about yourself. (Glue a small mirror to the 4" x 6" card.)

9. Find or write a poem about a dinosaur. (Place a dinosaur sticker on the card.)

10. Write a poem about your favorite cartoon or movie character. (Cut and glue on a picture of current cartoon or movie personalities.)

11. Write a poem about your favorite movie star. (Cut and glue on a picture of a familiar movie star.)

12. Write a poem about any member of your family.

13. Find or write a poem about insects or bugs.

14. Write a poem about your hobby or things you collect.

15. Write a poem about what you'd like to be when you grow up.

16. Write a poem about a favorite storybook character.

17. Write a poem about a favorite vacation place you have visited.

18. Write a poem about your favorite meal or dessert.

19. Find or write a funny poem.

20. Write a poem about what you like at school.

21. Write a poem for an answering machine message.

22. Find or write a poem about an animal you would like to be.

23. Find or write a poem about your favorite summertime activity.

24. Find or write a poem about something scary or frightening.

25. Find or write a poem about a pet.

Store the poetivity cards in a 4"x 6" card holder (tin or colorful plastic) or contact papered box. Label the box "Poetivities." Students are to complete the poetivities on 4"x 6" record sheets, duplicated, cut out and placed in the box along with the poetivity task cards.

| Poetivity # _____ |
| --- |
| Name: _____ |
| Date: _____ |
| Poem: |

## Research Report

The final activity for the poetry learning station is a research report. Students will choose a poet from the "Poets to Pursue" list of names, prepare a brief biographical sketch, and read one or two poems. Each student will have an opportunity to share their report with the class during a designated time each week . In no time, students will become familiar with the style and writings of many poets and be an "expert" on the one they researched. Have students sign up on a list, next to a poet they will pursue: Ogden Nash, Robert Louis Stevenson, Gwendolyn Brooks, Shel Silverstein, A. A. Milne, Robert Frost, Emily Dickinson, Carl Sandburg, Lewis Carroll, Henry Wadsworth Longfellow, Alfred Lord Tennyson, Walter De La Mare, Nikki Giovanni, Charlotte Zolotow, Judith Viorst, Jack Prelutsky, Dr. Seuss, Jeff Moss, Lee Bennet Hopkins, Eve Merriam, Edward Lear, Rudyard Kipling, Edgar Allan Poe, Maurice Sendak, John Updike, William Butler Yeats, John Keats, William Wordsworth, Elizabeth Browning, Robert Lowell, T. S. Eliot, Robert Burns, Eloise Greenfield, D. H. Lawrence, Walt Whitman, William Blake, William Shakespeare, Dorothy Aldis, Aileen Fisher, X. J. Kennedy, Elizabeth Coatsworth, Arnold Lobel, Margaret Wise Brown, Percy Shelley.

## Poetry Center Assignment

The following "Poetry Center Assignment" sheet can be posted on a large sheet at the learning station, as well as made into an individual check list for each student to have in their file folder. Students can check off the activities as they complete them.

1. Memorize a poem and recite it to the class.
2. Write one poem for the class poem book.
3. Make your own poem book.
4. Choose and complete at least one "Animal Antics" task card.
5. Choose and complete at least one "Time-of-the-Year" task card.
6. Choose and complete at least one "Picture Poetry" task card.
7. Choose and complete at least two "Poetivity" task cards.
8. Choose and research a poet to share with the class.
9. Place your work in your student file folder.

## Poetry Pocket Shirt

For an added classroom visual, display a "poetry pocket shirt" on a hanger. This shirt is fashioned from a large T-shirt (any color) with four to five colorful, cotton fabric pockets sewn onto the front. The purpose is for students to write their favorite poems on 4"x 6" cards and place them in the pockets. You may choose to have students use the sample poems they found for their "Poets to Pursue" research project. Designate a specific time or spontaneous point during the day for a student to put on the poetry pocket shirt, pull out a poem (or two) and read to the class. Be sure, you take the opportunity to put the poetry pocket shirt on yourself to share your favorite poems with the class. For another visual, create a whimsical poetry puppet character out of a kneesock. Decorate the worm-like, creature with pom-pom eyes, pipe-cleaner antennae, a bow tie and other clever touches. Pull the sock up your arm, tucking the end excess between your top four fingers and thumb to resemble a mouth. This puppet's name is "Longfellow." Allow students to wear Longfellow as they read the selected poems from the poetry pocket shirt. For fun students may want to read the poem for Longfellow to lip sync.

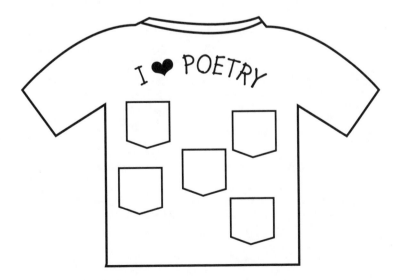

 Activity Fourteen

# Haiku and Senryu

Haiku is a three-line, unrhymed Japanese poem that is usually about nature. The first and third lines must have five syllables, while the second line must have seven (5,7,5). The senryu is a poem which follows the haiku form, but does not have to be about nature. Here are some sample haiku:

(5) Yellow daffodils          (5) Fall is coming soon

(7) Fragrant, frilly, nectar cup          (7) Swirl and twirl the leaves go 'round

(5) A gorgeous bouquet.          (5) The trees shiver cold.

Support students in their efforts to write haiku. First, brainstorm and list on chart paper nature topics that students can choose to write about, such as: sunset, earthquake, hurricane, thunderstorm, rainbow, waterfall, beach, sunrise, blizzard, clouds, wolf, desert, giraffe, cornfield, goldfish, tulips, wildflowers. Assist students in writing haiku poems by providing some of the words, for instance:

(5) Flash and thunderstorm          (5) Sunshine tan me brown.

(7) _____          (7) _____

(5) All is quiet now.          (5) So instead I'm red.

Try filling in the words to these senryu poems:

(5) School begins today          (5) It's cluttered, messy

(7) _____          (7) _____

(5) Boy, am I sleepy.          (5) But it's my bedroom.

Allow independent students time to create their own haiku and senryu poems. Ask students to share them orally.

## Activity Fifteen

# Compare and Contrast

Jane Yolen chose several poets and put together an anthology of poems that depict the sights, sounds and energy of the city titled *Sky Scrape/City Scape*. This book makes a great springboard into a compare/contrast theme between city and country life. To build background, you may want to explore other books on this topic and make them available in your classroom.

---

**Additional Resources About the City:**

Crews, Nina. *One Hot Summer Day*. Greenwillow Books, 1995.

DiSalvo, Ryan and Dyanne. *City Green*. Morrow Junior, 1994.

Hurwitz, Johanna. *Busybody Nora*. Penguin, 1976.

Keats, Ezra Jack. *Goggles*. Simon & Schuster, 1969.

Martin, Bill Jr. *Barn Dance*. Henry Holt, 1986.

O'Connor, Jane. *Molly the Brave and Me*. Random House, 1990.

Rylant, Cynthia. *The Blue Hill Meadows*. Harcourt Brace, 1997.

Schecter, Ellen. *Country Mouse and the City Mouse*. Gareth Stevens, 1996.

---

## Active Organizer Game

After enjoying several poems from *Sky Scrape/City Scape* and various literature links, enjoy a new activity called "Active Organizer" game (as opposed to a graphic organizer, which is a paper and pencil activity using a picture graph to organize information). In advance, cut a 12"x 18" sheet of colored construction paper in thirds. With a black marker, label one strip with the topic "country life," one with "city life," and the last with "common to both." Also, cut several 1"x 18" linking strips from colored construction paper. Tape one topic strip in the left corner of your classroom, one in the right corner, and the "common to both" strip in the front of the classroom. Divide your class into three groups, assigning them each a topic strip. Students should get into their groups and brainstorm words that would fit their assigned topic. Ask one student in the group to be a recorder and write the words on 3"x 5" cards with a black marker. Allow students about ten to fifteen minutes to complete this task. The following words may be helpful:

### City life

skyscrapers, highways, traffic jams, buses, subways, museums, sports arenas, smog, apartment buildings, factories, smokestacks, taxis, fire escapes, graffiti, sidewalks, parks, fountains, traffic lights

### Country life

barns, pastures, cows, horses, windmills, cornfields, manure, tractors, vegetable garden, flower garden, relaxed, fresh air, ponds, streams, stone fences, rolling hills, silos, electric fences, ducks, geese, pigs, chickens, hay

---

## Common to both

school buses, dogs, cats, gardens, restaurants, airports, fire station, ambulance, policeman

After students finishing recording words on the 3"x 5" cards ask them to tape or glue the linking strips behind the index cards to hang from their topic strip on the wall. They may wish to make two or three columns of word cards. Ask each group to take turns reading off the index cards to the class, adding other word suggestions that might not have been recorded. Extend this activity by encouraging students to illustrate city and country life and displaying their pictures around the topic strip and word cards on the wall in your classroom.

Wrap up this activity by sharing my follow-up sequel to the well-known story about the visit of the country mouse to the city. It begins on the next page and is titled "Country Cousins, City Cousins."

### Country Cousins, City Cousins

One evening, Country Mouse leaned back in his chair patting his bulging belly. "Well children, where shall we take a summer vacation this year?" Father Mouse gazed around the dinner table.

"Let's visit our cousins in the big city," shouted the mice children. "We've never been there before."

Father Mouse turned pale gray. "I… I visited my city cousin years ago, before you were born," he said, "we were chased by cats and people. I decided it was no place for a family," Father Mouse shuddered.

"But Dad, what's the city like? Couldn't we go? Please?" The mice surrounded their father's chair.

"Perhaps it's safer now, dear," said Mother Mouse. "We've never seen your cousin's family."

"True…," said Father Mouse stroking his whiskers.

"Does that mean 'yes'? When can we go?" the mice shouted.

Father Mouse nodded slowly, "I'm still afraid. But you need to see for yourself."

Early the next morning, suitcases in hand, Country Mouse and his family leaped on a bus and rode to the city. Finally, they reached the eleventh floor of a huge apartment building. Father rang the doorbell. "My, things have changed!" said Father Mouse looking over his shoulder for stray cats.

Suddenly, the door swung open. "Cousin!" City Mouse exclaimed, "it's wonderful to see you. Please come in." City Mouse led the way into the huge living room, where his family sat watching a Mickey Mouse movie on a big screen TV. The Country mice stood wide-eyed.

"Darling, this is my cousin and his family," said City Mouse. "They've come all the way from the country to visit us."

"Would you like something to eat?" asked Mrs. City Mouse. "You must be starved from your long trip."

"Yes, thank you," said Mrs. Country Mouse as she followed her to the kitchen.

"C'mon, we'll show you our computer games!" The City Mouse children led their cousins to the game room.

"Well, cousin, what brings you to the city? After the last visit, I thought you would never return," said City Mouse chuckling. "Remember when we got cornered by the old tabby?"

"How could I forget!" Country Mouse sighed. "Our children wanted to meet their cousins," said Country Mouse, "We also want to teach them the ways of the world." Country Mouse tapped his fingers on the lamp table.

"Cousin, you seem a bit nervous," said City Mouse.

"Do you still have cats here?" said Country Mouse. His voice shook.

"No, of course not! We don't have to worry about finding enough food or being eaten by hungry pets." He explained how he inherited his great-grandfather's 'flea collar alarm' business. "This new invention is better than putting a bell around the cat's neck," City Mouse boasted. "A secret sonar hooked to each flea collar warns mice of cat danger."

"Fascinating!" a much happier Country Mouse replied.

The wives returned with cheese and cracker snacks. They all nibbled and laughed as they shared family stories.

Soon it was bedtime. The Country Mouse family tried to sleep. But outside their window trucks honked, fire engines clanged and ambulance sirens blared. "I sure miss the sounds of peepers and crickets," whispered Mrs. Country Mouse to her husband.

In the morning, everyone gathered at the breakfast table. "Just look at the beautiful view from the window," said Mrs. City Mouse. "I just love the sight of the tall skyscrapers against the hazy, blue sky."

Mrs. Country Mouse nodded as she thought of the colorful wildflowers, a creek and clear blue sky in her own backyard at home. She smiled.

"Cousin, would you and your family like to do some sightseeing today?" City Mouse unfolded the tour maps in his lap.

"Sightseeing?" asked Country Mouse.

City Mouse continued, "First of all, you'll love the view from the top of Triplet Towers," said City Mouse pointing to the map. "And of course, a visit to the big city isn't complete until you've been to a baseball game at Yankee Doodle Stadium."

"Mom, Dad, this is going to be the best day ever!" sang the Country children.

All day, the mouse families toured the big city.

That evening, exhausted, they piled into the elevator for the eleventh floor apartment. In minutes, they were sound asleep in their beds.

The next morning the Country Mouse and his family packed their suitcases to leave for the country.

"We've enjoyed our visit to the big city. Thank you!" said Mrs. Country Mouse as she hugged Mrs. City Mouse.

"We're so glad you came," said Mrs. City Mouse. "Next time plan to stay longer. There's so much more to see."

"Oh, it's so good to be home," said Mrs. Country Mouse as she opened the squeaky gate that surrounded their sturdy stump house. "It's great to visit the city, but I still love the country best."

"Dad, could we go back to visit next year?" asked the mice children.

"Maybe," said Father Mouse happily. "I sure would like to see the Museum of Natural Mousetory."

 Activity Sixteen

# Free Verse

The beauty of writing free verse poems is there are no rules. They are an original poem of your own design and about any topic. Lines can be long or short, rhymed or unrhymed. Encourage your students to write in the free verse style. Tell them to begin by writing about what they know; family experiences, vacations, pets, hobbies and special people in their lives make great topics for free verse poems. Here's an example from my family, and a couple from a student:

### Gramma's Hugs and Kisses

When we visit Gramma
I just can't wait to leave.
For Gramma's hugs are strong and tight
That I can hardly breathe.

When Gramma grabs my face to plant
A kiss upon my cheek.
She makes a sound so loud and long,
A noisy, sucking squeak.

When we visit Gramma
I go with sickening dread.
I wish that she would kiss my dog
And shake my hand instead.

### Fall Fun

**by Mike Hoff, age 10**

It was a pretty day in the fall.
The wind blew through the trees.
Daddy and I had a ball catching leaves.

### Rotten

**by Mike Hoff, age 10**

My cat sleeps 24 hours a day.
And always, always gets her way.
She doesn't like the dog you see,
And hates getting put O-U-T.
She is very rotten indeed.
My whole family all agrees.

If students need additional ideas to create their own free verse poems, supply topics for them to choose from. Here are just a few:

1. On Thanksgiving (my birthday, Christmas), I ate too much …

2. Someday, I'd like to be …

3. I have hundreds of baseball cards (coins, matchbox cars, arrowheads) …

4. My best subject is art (math, science, music, lunch) …

5. No one knows my secret …

6. You won't believe what I found (saw, heard, bought) …

7. I love to read about space aliens (monsters, horses, volcanoes) …

8. For my birthday, I got …

Reading and writing poetry can be lots of fun. It will draw some students more than others, of course, but if you include it throughout your curriculum, wherever possible, students will learn to appreciate it and not be afraid of it.

 Activity Seventeen

# Absurdities

*Webster's Dictionary* defines an absurdity as something ridiculous, not possible, or just plain nonsense. Your students will enjoy the absurd and ridiculous poems found in Jane Yolen's book, *How Beastly*. Whether it's poems describing impossible antics, crazy things that happen to people, making animals come alive or combining animal traits for an outrageous outcome, people of all ages seem to enjoy a touch of nonsense. Perhaps Yolen collected, studied and experimented with scores of animal pictures before she created her "freaks of nature" book. These poems are full of creative "animal mix-ups" that could easily entice students to try drawing and writing some of their own.

First of all, point out some poems from *How Beastly* that show word plays and nonsense words, such as: "The Crocodial," "The Fanger," "The Porcupin," and "The Buffalo." Students can begin to see that almost anything goes in writing nonsense poems.

Have some fun with your students by checking to see if they know an absurdity when they hear it. The following exercises will steer your students into a nonsense mode, plus, give them some ideas for writing nonsense poems for Activity 19.

## Absurdity Exercises

Write a capital letter "A" on a 3"x 5" card for each student in your classroom. Pass the cards out. Ask students to listen carefully as you repeat phrases. If the phrase is an "absurdity," ask students to hold up their "A" index card. Read each phrase below:

### Exercise #1
- singing chickens (A)
- hungry crocodiles
- oinking cows (A)
- a 7,000 pound woman (A)
- a purple aardvark (A)
- sausage pizza
- surfing on skiis (A)
- a dog with feathers (A)
- a circus clown
- an old woman who lives in a shoe (A)
- a crazy quilt
- a roll away bed
- a painted turtle
- a talking ghost (A)
- a the cow jumped over the moon (A)

### Exercise #2
Ask students to listen carefully to the following sentences. Each of them make sense. The object is to "change *one* word, to make them absurd." Read a sentence, then call on a student to repeat the sentence with the one word change.

- The bird flew through the sky.
- The cow ran out to the pasture.
- Please go wash your hands.
- My dog buried a bone.
- I fell asleep in the chair.
- The girls picked apples off the tree.
- He put the popsicles in the freezer.
- I like to rake up the fall leaves.
- I planted flowers in my garden.
- I spent the summer painting the house.

For further reading, compare other author/poets that write nonsense poems, such as: Shel Silverstein, Jack Prelutsky, Jeff Moss, Arnold Lobel, Edward Lear, Dr. Seuss, and X.J. Kennedy.

# Nonsense Poems

Nonsense poems do not follow any special form, nor do they need to rhyme. After reading, building up background and collecting ideas for nonsense poems, invite students to experiment and create some of their own. If they wish to combine animal features, write about unusual events, people or places, allow them time to brainstorm independently, or pick a partner to collaborate with. You may wish to display and read the following actual student samples to motivate your class:

### I Have a Cow
**by Arthur Schad, age 10**

I have a cow named Sue.
She lives in a palace called "Moo."
She likes to wear shoes.
She likes to walk in the field all day.
Now her shoes are covered with moo-newer!

### The Boy Who Was Flying a Kite
**by Kyle Collins, age 11**

There was a boy flying a kite
In the night
And it was not very bright.

### The Shoe Tree
**by Melissa Torzon, age 10**

My puppy took my slippers and buried them
In the backyard.
He left them there, for eons, while beside
Them he stood guard.
One day it happened, a new tree tall and
Bold broke through the ground and blossomed.
There were no leaves on this new tree.
It looked very strange.
As leathery protrusions
Declared a colorful range
Of dockers, slip-ons, and sneakers,
There were sandles with open-toes.
Even high-heels, thongs and flippers.
Every kind of shoe that grows.
But not one pair of slippers
Did that tree in the yard sprout.
So I scolded my little puppy
For making me do without.

### There Once Was a Deer
**by Rex Walker, age 11**

There once was a deer
That had no fear
And he didn't know how to hear well.

In the forest at night
He was always a-fright
And his story is awful to tell.

He was strolling along
Just singing a song
About Bambi and Flower and Thumper.

When all of a sudden
Along came a car
And this deer now adorns a Ford bumper.

### There Once Was a Man
**by Emily Ferguson, age 11**

There once was a man
Who had a lamb.
The lamb had a cramp
Which made him stamp
And do a dance
All the way to France.

### I Had a Friend
**by Emily Ferguson, age 11**

I had a friend
Whose name was Ben.
We loved to sit and play.

We'd stand on our heads
And jump on our beds
And giggle the day away.

 Activity Nineteen

# Skill Draw

After reading the poems and enjoying the photographs in Jane Yolen's book titled, *Once Upon Ice*, engage your students in a brainstorming activity. Using a colored marker to record words on chart paper, ask students to list "words that remind them of winter." Possible suggestions are: icicles, frozen, blizzard, hockey, ice skating, snowmobiling, avalanche, skiing, ice fishing, sledding, slippery, snowflakes, snowplow, snowbanks, December, January, February, frost, iceberg, hibernation, flurries, wintry, snowsuit, boots, mittens, earmuffs, snowball, snowfort, sled, snowman, sleigh, Santa, presents, Christmas tree, caroling, reindeer.

## Winter Word Skill Activity

To make a skill activity using this list of "winter words," cut several 3"x5" index cards lengthwise and write a winter word on each card. Attach a piece of magnetic tape on the back of each card. Consider creating a snow shovel word holder as a wintertime visual for this activity. Stand a metal snow shovel in the corner of your classroom with the blade up. Attach the winter word cards to the blade. To complete this winter word skill activity, create skill strips which will ask students to perform a variety of specific tasks to do with the list of winter words that they brainstormed. These skill strips will include reading, language and writing skill ideas. Duplicate (twice), cut apart and glue the following skill strip ideas to fifteen, 5"x 8" cards cut in half lengthwise, for a total of 30 skill strips:

1. Write a free verse poem using five of the winter words.
2. Read a "wintertime" story and share a retelling of the story to the class.
3. List all the compound winter words and illustrate five of them.
4. Write a short story using 10 of the winter words.
5. List all the winter sports you can think of. Pick two favorites and tell why you like them.
6. Write a winter word tongue twister.
7. Find a winter poem, memorize it and share it with the class.
8. Write an acrostic poem using the word WINTER.
9. Write 10 fill-in the blank sentences, using 10 winter words.
10. Choose three winter words and write a list of rhyming words with each.
11. Choose 15 winter words and categorize them under three different topics.
12. Choose 20 winter words and put them in alphabetical order.
13. Find a winter/holiday song with five winter words in it and sing to the class.
14. Write 3 rhyming couplets using three winter words.
15. Using a thesaurus and/or dictionary, find 10 more words to add to the winter word list.

Place skill strips in a winter-themed mug or contact-papered can. Allow students to select skill strips and complete the task on the strip. Set aside time for students to share their work.

 Activity Twenty

# Triplets

A triplet is a three-line poem on any topic with two or three lines that rhyme. If you wish to stay with the winter theme from Activity 21, provide some writing ideas by discussing real or make-believe ways to use ice cubes, icicles, frost and snow. For instance:

**What can you do with ice cubes?**

stack them to make an ice castle, put them down someone's back, cool down your hot cocoa, put it on a bump on your head

**What can you do with icicles?**

build an icicle house, have a duel, make walrus teeth, string them together like prisms

**What can you do with frost?**

make thumb print creatures on a frosted window, breathe on a frosted window to make peek holes, scrape it off a window and form it into balls

**What can you do with snow?**

lay down in it and make snow angels, use it to make and freeze homemade ice cream, form it into blocks to build a snow fort, build a snowman

If these ideas don't trigger some triplet writing, move on to something more familiar, such as writing about members of your own family. Ask students to brainstorm on their own paper about family get-togethers, birthdays, vacations, happy times, silly times, sibling problems, pets, etc. Share the following triplets with your students to get their creative juices flowing.

**Two rhyming lines:**

### Brother

He yells and runs, grins and <u>hugs</u>.
He teases, laughs, gets dirty and <u>slugs</u>.
I'm talking about my brother!

### Huggle

When us kids are feeling cold,
We stand close, hug and <u>snuggle</u>.
So it's called our "<u>huggle</u>."

**Three rhyming lines:**

### Peas

Sit down and eat your <u>peas</u>.
I don't want to say it again, <u>please</u>.
No they won't give you a <u>disease</u>!

### Christmas Tree

"Let's go cut a Christmas <u>tree</u>!"
As I slipped and sprained my <u>knee</u>.
"Instead, you'll have to go on a shopping <u>spree</u>."

# Four Ws and Sentence Structure

Students will enjoy the rhyme and rhythm of Jane Yolen's book *An Invitation to the Butterfly Ball*. All of the animals, from one little mouse to ten porcupines, busied themselves by collecting or making appropriate clothing for the ball. "Knock. Knock. Who's come to call? An invitation to the Butterfly Ball."

An invitation card always lists the necessary information so the guest knows: who, what, where, and when. In the same way, the sentences in a story must answer those same questions in order to make the story flow, build the story plot, and entice the reader to keep reading.

### Build a Sentence Game

Students may need practice including the 4 Ws in their sentences and stories. Provide some small group practice by creating a "Build a Sentence" game board with a built-in spinner and four different sets of colored cards.

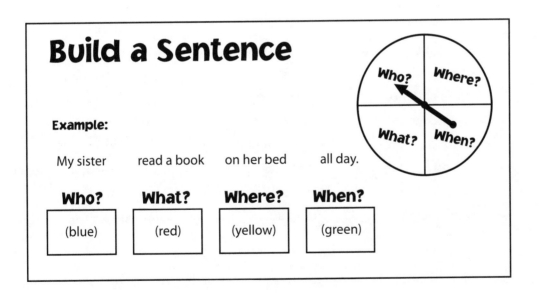

# Directions for Game Board

Cut a 22"x 28" piece of poster paper in half. With a marker, trace a circle in the upper, right corner of the game board to use for a spinner. Divide the circle into quarters and trace the lines with a marker. Cut out a cardboard arrow, hole punch the center and push a brad fastener through the arrow and game board, loosely enough for the arrow to spin, then bend the brad fastener. Cut out four sets of twenty-one 2" x 4" construction paper cards of four different colors (blue, red, yellow, green). Use one card of each color to mount on the game board labeled with: Who? (in blue), What? (in red), Where? (in yellow), and When? (in green). Write the following phrases on the cards:

| Who? cards (in blue): | What? Cards (in red): | Where? cards (in yellow): | When? cards (in green): |
|---|---|---|---|
| Those two dogs | popped a balloon | to their house | this morning. |
| The cowboys | rode their bicycles | in the air | last night. |
| Those children | played | in the race | every day. |
| The jogger | ran around | in the country | today. |
| The Brown family | were played | at the zoo | yesterday. |
| His sister | saw something strange | at the party | after hurting his ankle. |
| The farmer | dug a large hole | at the dance | this afternoon. |
| We | invited us | in the yard | about a year ago. |
| A small puppy | lost their mother | around his ranch | last spring. |
| Her grandma | was found | to the top of the trees | tomorrow night. |
| My dog | raked the leaves | in the field | all day. |
| The boys | read a story | at school | after supper. |
| Some children | ate too much ice cream | in the pasture | on Saturday. |
| The pilot | scampered | in the store | a little while ago. |
| The animals | built a big fence | in the neighbor's yard | during the rodeo. |
| The babies | enjoyed the concert | outdoors | during his flight. |
| That monkey | climbed | in the restaurant | yesterday evening. |
| Jane and Tom | formed a circle | in the field | while their mom shopped. |
| My parents | could not run | in school | all morning. |
| My pen pal | wrote a letter | in the barn | last week. |

Laminate all cards for durability. Write the directions on the back of the game board. How to play: Place the colored card sets face down on their corresponding color on the game board. The first player spins and takes the same colored card as that to which the spinner arrow points. The next player spins and takes one card. Play continues clockwise. When a player is able to make a complete sentence, he/she scores five points, provided he/she is able to read the entire sentence. The game continues until all the cards have been drawn. The player with the most points at the end of the game is the winner.

 Activity Twenty-two

# Limericks

A limerick is a five line, humorous poem with lines 1, 2 and 5 rhyming and each containing eight syllables, and lines 3 and 4 rhyming and each containing five syllables (aabba). Often limericks begin with: "There was a…" or "There once was a… ." It's very interesting to note that Edward Lear made limericks popular back in 1846 when he wrote his *Book of Nonsense*. This form of humorous verse is short but contains puns (plays on words) and has a catchy rhythm. The limerick was named after the city of Limerick, Ireland.

Read some sample limericks, including the one I've included here, to your class in preparation for them to create some of their own.

**Sample limerick**

Behold the African reptilian
His wrinkled skin looks quite sillian.
With legs long and slender
He's a credit to his gender.
He climbs with great strength and agilian.

Bill Higby

### ★ For Younger Students

For younger students, you may want to support their first attempts at writing limericks by providing some fill-in-the-blank verses. Your limerick examples could mention teachers, student names, class experiences and/or humorous anecdotes, as in the following:

There once was a _____ named Mrs. Potts
Who was green and _____ with spots.
She ate _____ and bread
She wore a _____ on her head,
And on her face were _____ dots.

There once was a _____ named Cathy,
Who was _____ and would not take a bathy.
She _____ in the dirt,
But _____ get hurt.
And she lived in a _____ on the pathy.

To keep limerick examples from year to year as a language lesson, write them on poster paper and decorate with pictures or stickers, or ask your school art teacher if she would illustrate these for your use in the classroom. To make a reusable, durable limerick big book, laminate the poster pages, punch holes in the top of each page, insert loose-leaf rings and turn it into a flip chart. Students can use a marker to fill-in-the-blanks. The marker can be removed with fingernail polish remover or rubbing alcohol and used over again. Clean off the marker before putting it away for the following school year to avoid leaving a permanent stain.

When your students understand the pattern of the limerick, it's sometimes fun to change or vary it slightly. For older students, start by providing the first two lines and encouraging them to fill in the rest:

There was an old man named Friday
Who washed his car every Saturday.

_____

_____

_____.

I have a poodle named Ker-choo
Who is always chewing my shoe.

_____

_____

_____.

 Activity Twenty-three

# Alliterative Qualities

Jane Yolen's *Elfabet* is a great example of elfish alphabetical alliteration. Each alphabet letter and accompanying text exhibits the super sounds of sameness that tempts the flexibility of the tongue. This book makes an appropriate read-aloud to introduce and teach students the alliterative qualities of literature. Alliteration is a poetic device that creates sound effects by stringing words together that have the same initial sound. For example: "A is for Acorn Elf, always acrobatic. B is for Bottle Elf, boldly balancing." Many students are familiar with tongue twisters, some of which can be lengthy and difficult to repeat. However, the challenge is to correctly enunciate each word and say it faster at the same time. That's what makes alliteration fun.

Another book that follows an alliterative pattern is *Dinorella* by Pamela Duncan Edwards. Students will enjoy this prehistoric version of the Cinderella fairy tale because it uses the letter D throughout all 32 pages. This picture book is also appropriate for a read-aloud at the intermediate level because of its challenging vocabulary. Such words as: dainty, dependable, droning, dismal, dazzle, declared, deafening, disturbance, dastardly, devour, digesting, dumbfounded, disbelief, detached, departed, doomed, dimwits, defended, delirious, dames, damsel, domestic, and distracted are a few of the many alliterative words. This story contains wonderful, descriptive words that fill your mind with visual images.

*Double Trouble in Walla Walla* is a very creative picture book written by Andrew Clements. This author uses alliteration, rhyme, repeated words and onomatopoeia (words which sound like the sound or action they describe, such as buzz, hiss, honk, etc.) to enhance the story plot. It's about an ordinary morning in Walla Walla until Lulu, her teacher, the school nurse, and the principal are all caught in a word warp, which makes them talk all "higgledy-piggledy." Again, students of all ages will enjoy this book, especially the intermediate students. The story theme and use of poetic language is a great writing motivator. It builds background for students to glean ideas from when writing their own pieces. As teachers, we need to support students in their writing by praising their efforts, building their confidence, and strengthening their background knowledge. Students need clear, visual and auditory examples of our writing expectations before they are given an assignment.

**Double Trouble in Walla Walla Game**

Using the "super duper" word combinations in *Double Trouble...*, I created a game board where each pathway space was labeled with story vocabulary such as Walla Walla, Lulu, nit-wit, higgledy-piggledy, tip-top, mish-mash, flip-flop, chitter-chatter, double trouble, itty-bitty, shilly-shally, dilly-dally, fancy-schmancy, yak-yak, trit-trot, hee hee, my my, eeka-freaka, uh oh, hubbub, tut-tut, razzle dazzle, lippity-loppity, jibber-jabber, helter-skelter, silly willy, hocus-pocus, topsy-turvy, jim-jams, yoo-hoo, pitter-patter, okey-dokey, howdy-doody, wasko-wacko, sing-song, fiddle-faddle, palsy-walsies, phony-baloney, flim-flam, tutti-frutti, jeepers-creepers, holy-moly—and these words are only in the first ten pages! Not only will this game stretch your students' phonic and decoding skills, but it will also enhance understanding and practice of poetic language at its extreme. It's just plain fun!

**How to play**

Follow the same general game directions as in activity 7, except when students land on the pathway space and cannot correctly identify the word, they have to move back one space until they can. Then they stay on that space until their next turn.

 Activity Twenty-four

# Alphabet Alliteration

After reading examples of alliterative literature (Activity 23), invite students to create an alliterative sentence using the first letter of their names. For example:

> Sarah sang her song so soft and sweet.
>
> David drew a dancing dinosaur on a sand dune.
>
> Ben brought brownies for his birthday today.

On chart paper, list each alphabet letter down the page, then list students' names next to the appropriate letter. You will have more than one child per letter and may not have students to cover other letters. Some students will complete this task quickly. Allow them to choose another letter, pick a name, and write an alliterative sentence, thus using all the letters of the alphabet. Give students time to illustrate their sentences, then laminate the pages, put them in ABC order, and bind the pages together for a class book titled, *ABC Alliteration*. You may wish to extend this activity by allowing students to write couplets or quatrains using alliteration and rhyme.

# Visual Images

Before reading Jane Yolen's *Welcome to the Green House*, set the stage with your students by discussing different kinds of "houses." Ask student to "visualize" and describe what a "greenhouse" is. Using chart paper, record all of their responses: e.g., a plastic, see-through house; a glass house for plants; a place to buy plants and trees; a plant nursery; a place where plants are in big pots; a place where mom buys plants for our garden. You may wish to carry on this visual image activity to include student descriptions of a treehouse, birdhouse, smokehouse, doghouse, boathouse, etc. Use a separate piece of chart paper for each "house" you discuss. Allow students time at the end of the day to look for magazine pictures or illustrate each of these "houses." Glue the picture at the top of each chart page you've discussed. Your wrap-up statement should define a "house" as a place where someone or something lives, stays or is stored.

Show students the front and back cover of Jane Yolen's book, *Welcome to the Green House*. Locate your "greenhouse" chart page and briefly review your description of a "greenhouse." Before reading the book text, slowly flip through each page of the book allowing students to make comments about what the pictures show. Then read the story. This may be the first exposure your primary students will have to the term "rain forest." But it's valuable background information for future studies they will encounter. More than ever, picture books are a great resource and can be used to prepare our students for upcoming themes and topics for reading and writing activities. The more exposure, discussion and application we can draw out of our young students, the more experience and knowledge they will have to build upon later. This book can be used as a teaching tool at all levels.

## ★ For Older Students

For older students, you may wish to expand the book's theme by naming and researching the different creatures that live in a rain forest: sloths, capuchins, snakes, toads, hummingbirds, lizards, silver fish, beetles, golden lion tamarins, toucans, wild pigs, herons, kinkajous, ocelots, etc.

## ★ For Younger Students

### Pom-Pom People

For younger students, you may wish to discuss the colors of the plants and animals that live in the rain forest. To reinforce color and color word recognition skills, make the following puppet visual, auditory and tactile activity. Purchase or recycle a pair of dark-colored gloves. Hot glue medium-sized pom-poms of ten different colors, (red, orange, yellow, green, blue, purple, brown, black, white and pink), one on top of each finger of the glove. Hot glue a pair of moveable eyes on each pom-pom, creating "pom-pom people." About a half an inch below the pom-pom, hot glue a small piece of Velcro. Cut out ten cardboard oval shapes, using the following pattern:

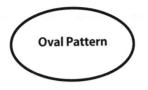

Oval Pattern

With a medium-fine black marker, write a color word on each cardboard oval. Laminate the cardboard. Using tacky glue, attach the matching Velcro strip to the back of each piece of cardboard.

## How to play

Gather students around you on the floor and place the cardboard ovals at your feet. Put the gloves on and repeat the following poem in a sing-song manner:

### *Pom-Pom People*

*(move fingers as the poem describes)*

Pom-pom people dance all day.
Pom-pom colors in bright array.

Pom-pom RED wiggle up, wiggle down.
Pom-pom PINK bend over like a frown.

Pom-pom ORANGE sway like a tree.
Pom-pom BROWN point your head at me.

Pom-pom YELLOW wiggle-jiggle 'round.
Pom-pom BLACK curl down like a mound.

Pom-pom GREEN stand straight and tall.
Pom-pom WHITE look at the wall.

Pom-pom BLUE there's nothing to do
So pom-pom PURPLE give a kiss to blue. (smack)

Pom-pom people dance all day.
Pom-pom colors in bright array.

Choose one student at a time to pick up a color word oval (lying on the floor at your feet) and match it to the same colored pom-pom puppet. Remind students to make the sound of the first letter they see on the color word oval, match it and stick it to the puppet. Place these "pom-pom people" gloves in a learning center for students to play with and match the colors to. For easy storage, place the color oval cards inside the glove and hold the gloves together with a clothespin.

# Picture Poems

Well in advance, make large poem cards to display around your classroom. Choose a variety of poems from various poets, then according to the theme of the poem, draw or find a pattern of the animal or object, trace it on an overhead transparency, and lastly, transfer the picture onto large poster paper. Color the drawing, write the poem in the center, laminate, then cut around the picture. (There are many publishing companies that sell pattern books for those of us who are artistically challenged.) Build up a supply of large poetry cards that will cover holidays throughout the year as well as zoo animals, farm animals, pets and various school themes. The more poetry becomes a part of your everyday reading and enjoyment the more natural it will be for your students to read it, write it and appreciate it. Use the following poems and illustrations as a starter for your poetry-picture card collection:

**One Sock, Two Socks**
**by Cheryl Potts**

One sock,
Two socks,
Red socks,
Blue socks,
New socks,
Old socks,
Dull socks,
Bold socks,
Lost socks,
Found socks,
Plaid socks,
Loud socks,
Missed socks,
Gone socks,
No socks,
Sockless!

**My Cat**
**by Cheryl Potts**

My cat is white with big brown spots
Her feet have seven toes.
She swats the dog when mealtime comes
The cat is boss, he knows.

**Pasta**
**by Cheryl Potts**

Pasta, pasta
Boiling fasta.
I'm so hungry
It won't lasta.
Cool it, serve it.
Tasty, tasty.
Gobble down.
Hasty, hasty.
Fill the tummy.
Yummy, yummy!
Ate too much.
Dummy, dummy!

## Student Picture Poems

After students have done a rough draft, revision and final copy of their poems, allow them to make their own poetry picture cards to display the poems they've written. Have several transparencies made up ahead that picture cats, dogs, rabbits, cows, horses, dinosaurs, bears, elephants, houses, cars, buses, crayons, books, etc. In order to anticipate what animals or objects children may write about or to narrow their focus and give them ideas, ask students to fill out the following survey and return it.

## Interest Survey

Name_____

Date_____

1.  My favorite dessert._____
2.  My favorite meal._____
3.  I have a pet_____
4.  Name the people in your family._____
5.  My favorite sport or hobby._____
6.  When I visit the zoo, my favorite animal is_____
7.  What I do after school and on weekends. _____ _____
8.  I like to read about_____
9.  What I like about school._____
10. What I'd like to be when I grow up._____

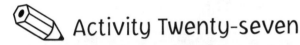 Activity Twenty-seven

# Oral Reading Fluency

Jane Yolen's book titled *Weather Report* is an anthology of poems covering all types of weather and seasons, written by several authors. Share some of these poems with your students. Ask them to brainstorm and list on chart paper different weather conditions the poems described, plus others that are not mentioned. For instance: sun, rain, cloudy, snow, wind, fog, sleet, hail, thunderstorms, droughts, tornadoes, hurricanes, cyclones, typhoons. Collect more weather poems from poetry books to begin a collection of weather poems for your classroom library. The following are suggestions: *The Random House Book of Poetry for Children* (Random House, 1983) selected by Jack Prelutsky. This book includes poems such as "The Wind" by James Reeves, "Who Has Seen the Wind" by Christina Rossetti, "Rain Clouds" by Elizabeth-Ellen Long, "To Walk in Warm Rain" by David McCord, "When All the World is Full of Snow" by N.M. Bodecker, and many more. *Sing a Song of Popcorn.* (Scholastic, 1988) selected by Beatrice Schenk de Regniers. This book includes poems such as "Weather" by Marchette Chute, "Rain" by Robert Louis Stevenson, "April Rain Song" by Langston Hughes, and "Snowflakes" by David McCord.

Categorize all the weather poems into different sections. Illustrate a weather page to begin each section of the weather poem book. For instance, the "Sunny Day" poem section could be illustrated with a huge yellow construction paper sun on a light blue background. The "Snow" section could be illustrated with a white paper snowflake on a dark blue background. Allow students time to create these weather section pages, then laminate. Students may wish to use their best penmanship and duplicate their favorite poem page, being sure to include the poet's name. Also encourage students to write their own weather poems to add to the weather book. I wrote the two poems that follow which you may add to your collection:

## The Snow Just Never Ends

Well, the snow just never ends.
It goes on and on my friends.
Some people started saying that
The snow'd be melting soon.
Another storm just hit us
We'll be shoveling until June.

Well, the snow just never ends.
It goes on and on my friends.
Some people tired of snow and cold
Are getting quite depressed.
The boots, the mittens, scarves and hats
Deserve a little rest.

Well, the snow just never ends.
It goes on and on my friends.
Some people caught spring fever
When last week it got so warm (40).
But now they're back inside the house
And waiting out a storm.

Well, the snow just never ends.
It goes on and on my friends…

## Hooray!

Hooray for the ice!
Hooray for the snow!
The roads are all plowed, as a rule.

Hooray for the wind!
Hooray for the sleet!
Today, they have cancelled school!

Use three loose-leaf rings to bind this weather poem book together, so more pages can be added at any time. Each morning, ask for one or two volunteers to choose and read a poem orally. Pick poems that match the weather for the day. As poems are re-read and enjoyed from day to day, student's oral reading confidence will grow. When a reluctant reader chooses a poem that's been read before (because it's a "safe" one to read), encourage and praise his or her efforts. Oral reading fluency improves through practice and praise.

Try a variation on the previous activity. Create a radio station in your classroom. Set up a table with a table top microphone and stand (real or homemade). Add a record player, tape deck, CD player, or other sound equipment (for looks) to create the desired effect. Make up call letters and frequency numbers to create a "live" radio broadcast. Since I teach in the A.P.W. School District, our radio station call letters are: "WAPW, 107.1 on your radio dial." As a radio announcer, I used to practice the news and weather forecasts before I read them over the air. This was necessary to avoid pronunciation errors with difficult names or places. If you are fortunate to have a radio station in your area, videotape or visit a live broadcast. Use your library resources to locate books on the role of a disc jockey, radio announcer, etc. This will give your students some background knowledge and understanding of radio jargon and format. Before visiting a radio station, you may want to call the station manager and ask her to save you old copies of the world and national news and weather reports that could be used for your classroom broadcast. The more authentic the material, the more motivated your students will be to rehearse (oral reading fluency) the news and weather for their listening audience (the class). Your classroom radio program log (outline for your radio program) could look something like this:

1. Announcer ID/Station ID

2. Time/Weather intro

3. Local Advertisement (commercial)

4. Weather Report

5. Time/Station and Announcer ID

6. Song

## Radio Broadcast

*Before every news or weather broadcast the radio announcer identifies himself and the radio station (Station ID).*

**Anncr:**   Good morning, this is _____ (name of announcer), from the newsroom of WAPW, 107.1 FM radio with the news and weather forecast. The time now is 10:56 a.m. Stay tuned for the weather report right after this message.

*Use the same or different student to read this sample advertisement from a local business:*

**Anncr:**   Come in for a shave and a haircut at Barbaroli's Barbershop. Charlie has everything he needs to make you suave and debonair. From the latest men's hair styles to the colognes of France. He can make you look and smell like a million bucks. Don't forget, Charlie Barbaroli's Barbershop, the corner of Rt. 31 and 104, open Monday through Saturday, from nine to five. Call 123-SNIP, that's 123-7647 for your appointment today. Walk-ins are welcome.

*The following is a sample business ad for two students to read:*

**Dan:**   Yes sir, Fred, at Cackleberry's Used Car Sales they mean what they say, that "folks can rely on what they buy… "

**Fred:** That's good! I've got a friend who's looking for a used car in excellent condition with low mileage.

**Dan:** Low mileage, eh? Well, Jerry and Terry Cackleberry have a car on the lot now that fits that description! This car has less than 10,000 miles and is only five years old!

**Fred:** Don't tell me that it was owned by a little old lady who only drove it on Sundays!

**Dan:** How did you know? You're right, it belonged to "Cannonball Clara." She only drove it in the stock car races on Sundays.

**Fred:** Oh!

**Dan:** Yeah! It's a great low mileage car if you don't mind a stripped down model with roll bars.

**Fred:** Don't listen to ole' Daniel, now folks, head on over to Cackleberry's Used Cars on Rt. 22, Waterloo, and get the best automobile buys in the area. That's Cackleberry's Used Cars, Rt. 22, in Waterloo.

**Anncr:** Now, for a look at today's weather: Today will be mostly sunny with periods of light rain. The highs will be in the 40s, with the chance of precipitation at twenty percent. The current temperature is 43 degrees. The time now is 11:01 a.m. This has been the WAPW weather forecast for our listening area, I'm _____ (name of announcer).

If you wish to continue programming, allow students an opportunity to introduce a song by its title (record, tape, CD) and artist. Then play the song.

This activity could be extended into reading your school morning announcements as though it were on radio. You might even invite a guest disc jockey to come and do a demonstration on your mock radio station.

 Activity Twenty-eight

# Concrete Poems

A concrete poem is a picture poem without the lines. Students may enjoy creating and writing this type of short poem because it doesn't have to rhyme. The letters and words trace the movement of an object or the outline shape of an object. Share the following poems with your students. They show the movement of an object:

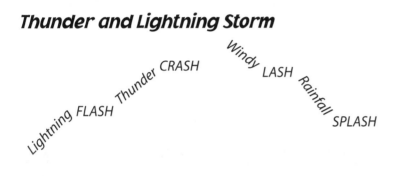

### Thunder and Lightning Storm

Lightning FLASH Thunder CRASH Windy LASH Rainfall SPLASH

### A Brief Rain

Gentle rain Misty drops Sprinkles softly Then it Stops!

Support students in their attempts to write concrete poems by listing some word phrases. Then ask them to write a short concrete poem that shows the movement of an object. Here are some ideas to experiment with: popcorn popping, a kangaroo hopping, a spaceship taking off, a snake slithering, a pond rippling, a hot shower, skiing down a slope, a waterfall.

Concrete poems also follow the outline of an object. You may wish to draw a very light pencil sketch of the object before putting the words in place. For example:

### The Staircase

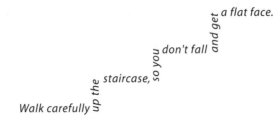

Walk carefully up the staircase, so you don't fall and get a flat face.

## a Kite

As a class, brainstorm a list of simple objects (topics) that would make effective concrete poems. Think of words or phrases that support, describe, or define that object, then, organize them into the outline shape of the object. For instance: butterfly, house, guitar, truck, school bus, bicycle, horse, dog, sneaker, fishing pole, ladder, giraffe, airplane, swing set, circus tent, hammer, football

## Fish

12"
bass
summertime
pond
lure
all day

Encourage your students to choose a topic and complete a concrete poem to share with the class. Compile the collection of poems into a classroom book titled, "Concrete Poems." On the book cover, draw a pile of gray concrete blocks. Inside each block list titles of the poems your students created. Keep the student-made book in easy reach for children to read, reread and enjoy.

# The Finishing Touches

This activity is about writing, rewriting, rereading, reviewing, rethinking, rearranging, repairing, restructuring, reevaluating, editing, tightening, sharpening, smoothing, pruning, polishing, punching up, amending, altering, eliminating, transposing, expanding, condensing, connecting, unifying, and perfecting. A one-word summary for the above is revision. Every quality written piece of work needs to be revised. This is one phase of the writing process approach.

After writing poems or stories, students (and teachers) need to give their pieces a "day to rest." Never think the first writing is your best work. The following day, writers should take a fresh look at their poem or story and decide if any changes need to be made. Good writers read their work with a critical eye, several times, to be sure it says exactly what they intended it to say. If students take writing seriously, they will understand that the purpose of writing is to communicate with the reader. The reader could be a teacher, a friend, your grandmother or students in the classroom. Whoever the reader may be, finished (or published) writing should always be your best effort. There are several "fine tuning" reminders to look for. Read your writing piece and respond to the following questions:

1. Have I stuck to one subject or topic?

2. Did I use worn-out cliches, tired or boring words or phrases?

3. Does my title reflect the mood or feeling of the poem or story?

4. Do the words of my writing piece create a visual image in my mind?

5. Have I used descriptive, active or picturesque words?

6. Do my ideas, words, sentences, or paragraphs flow in a steady manner?

7. Have I been clear, concise and to the point?

8. Do my nouns and verbs agree?

9. Are my verb tenses consistent?

10. Are my ideas, facts, information in correct, logical sentences?

11. Have I repeated the same word or words too many times?

12. Have I created a strong beginning to my poem or story?

13. Have I written an effective, logical, or creative ending?

14. Have I varied the length of my sentences and paragraphs?

15. Have I properly punctuated and not over-used certain punctuation marks?

16. Did I check the spelling of words for which I'm unsure?

17. Have I used words that would appeal to my five senses?

18. Am I satisfied with my story or poem as a whole? Does it convey my message?

19. Is my piece complete? Do I need to say more?

Read your writing piece to a friend. Listen and thank them for their opinions or ideas.

# Summary

| Form | Characteristics |
|------|-----------------|
| couplets | 2 lines with end rhyme |
| triplets | 3 lines with 2–3 lines that rhyme |
| haiku | unrhymed, 3 line, 5–7–5 syllable pattern about nature |
| senryu | unrhymed, 3 line, 5–7–5 syllable pattern about any topic |
| quatrain | 4 line poem with aabb or abcb rhyme scheme |
| clerihew | 4 line poem with aabb rhyme scheme, using person's name as the last word in the first line |
| tanka | unrhymed, 5 line, 5–7–5–7–7 syllable pattern about seasons or nature |
| cinquain | unrhymed, 5 line, with specific rules:<br>Line 1: 1 word topic (noun)<br>Line 2: 2 adjectives (describing line 1)<br>Line 3: 3 action words<br>Line 4: 4 words expressing feeling about topic<br>Line 5: 1 word, synonym for line 1 |
| limerick | 5 line, humorous poem with aabba rhyme scheme |
| Diamonte | unrhymed, 7 line poem shaped like a diamond with specific rules:<br>Line 1: 1 word topic (noun)<br>Line 2: 2 words describing topic (adjectives)<br>Line 3: 3 action words (verbs)<br>Line 4: 4 words (nouns), the first two relate to the topic of line 1, the last two relate to the topic of line 7<br>Line 5: 3 action words (verbs) relating to the topic of line 7<br>Line 6: 2 words describing the topic of line 7<br>Line 7: 1 word (noun) opposite of line 1 |
| Acrostic | unrhymed with the first letter of each line spelling out the topic vertically |
| Free Verse | follows no specific rules |
| Nonsense | topic needs to be absurd or ridiculous, follows no other specific rules |

# Teacher Resources

Chirinian, Helene. *Learning About Poetry*. Frank Schaffer, 1983.

Gruber, Sue and Barbara. *Using Poetry*. Frank Schaffer, 1990.

Lewis, Peggy Hapke. *Writing Poetry*. McDonald, 1993.

Luetje, Carolyn and Quinn, Carol. *Poem Patterns*. Edupress, 1988.

Prusinski, Shirley. *Writing Poems*. Remedia, 1996.

Simpson, Carol. *Daily Poetry*. GoodYear, 1995.

Sweeney, Jacqueline. *Teaching Poetry*. Scholastic, 1993.

Wainwright, James. *Poetivities Intermediate* and *Poetivities Primary*. Good Apple, 1989.